SOUND BITES

Quotes for our times

This book is inspirational. Buy it!
Lenny Henry

Whatever you can do
or dream you can do, begin it.
Boldness has genius, power
and magic in it.
Begin it now.

SOUND BITES

Quotes for our times

Compiled by **New Internationalist**

Illustrations by Korky Paul

First published in the UK by
New Internationalist Publications Ltd
55 Rectory Road
Oxford OX4 1BW UK

Printed in United Kingdom by
T. J. International Ltd, Padstow, Cornwall

British Library Cataloguing-in-Publication Data.
A catalogue record for this book is available from the British Library.
ISBN 1–869847–31–8

Acknowledgements

In compiling this collection of quotations and sayings we have gathered material from the **New Internationalist** magazine and Almanac, newspapers, TV/radio and internet, as well as from NI subscribers who kindly sent in their contributions. Special thanks to Henry W Allan, John D Anderson, S Berard, Tamara Bond, Chas Booth, Howard Brandwood, Ewan Bryce, LJ Clarke, Matthew Clarke, Dermot Daley, Peter Davis, Steve Dunne, Julie Foreman, Vincent Gainey, Sophie Gebreyes, M Gibson, Tony Goodchild, Mike Harper, Juergen Holst, Ron Houlihan, SA Jayawardene, Kim Kilvington, Rafael Kimberley-Bowen, Ann Knight, Maria Kugelmann, Bill Latona, Virge MacLeod, Noel Mahon, Rick McDaniel, Hugh McKinley, Kathleen Naylor, John Neal, Kath O'Kane, Rosemary Pearce, Andrew Pinney, Beric Raymond Barker, Matthew Shepherd, Bridgitte Tadrosse, Norman Taylor, Federico Tibone, Sara Trevillion, Mandy Truong, Denis Underwood, Sue Upton. Books consulted include *Genesis* Eduardo Galeano (Methuen 1986); *Prisoners of Jebs* Ken Saro-Wiwa (Saros International Publishers 1988); *Mahi's Story* (The Women's Press 1995); *The Education of the Little Tree* Forest Carter; *Daughters of Africa* Ed. Margaret Busby (Vintage 1993); *Toward the Splendid City* Pablo Neruda; *Zen Mind, Beginner's Mind* Shunryu Suzuki; *The Lucky Chance* Aphra Benn; *This be the Verse* Philip Larkin; *Deschooling Society* Ivan Illich (1971); *Tales of Tenderness and Power* Bessie Head (Heinemann 1990); *The Paradox of Economic Growth and Inequity* Kenneth Boulding; *Small is Beautiful* EF Schumacher; *Naked Truth and Veiled Allusions* Minna Antrim (1902); *Father You Gave Us the Dreaming* Djiniyini Gondarra; *The Fall of the Imam* Nawal el Saadawi (Minerva 1989); *Open Door* Luisa Valenzuela (Serpent's Tail 1992); *These are not sweet girls* Ed. Majorie Agosin (White Pine Press 1994); *The autobiography of Margot Asquith*; *Possessing the Secret of Joy* Alice Walker; *The Invisible Man* Ralph Ellison; *Sixth Meditation* René Descartes; *Women in Brazil* (Latin American Bureau 1994); *From Purdah to Parliament* Shaista Ikramullah (1963); *Breaking the Glass Ceiling* Ann M Morris et al (Addison-Wesley 1987); *Caribbean Poetry* (Heinemann 1992); *The Unsex'd Females: A Poem* Richard Polwhele; *We sinful women* Ed. Rukhsana Ahmad (The Women's Press 1991); *A Vindication of the Rights of Woman* Mary Wollstonecraft; *Wailing the Dead to Sleep* Lucinda Roy (Bogle-L'Ouverture 1988); *Little Women* Louisa M Alcott; *History of Woman Suffrage* (sic) Elizabeth Cady Stanton; *My Own Story* Emmeline Pankhurst (c 1908); *Decline and Fall* Evelyn Waugh (Penguin 1928); *Cimarron* Edna Ferber (1929); *Goodbye to All That* Robert Graves (1929); *Declaration des droits de la femme et la citoyenne* Olympe de Gouges (1791); *The Women's History of the World* Rosalind Miles; *The Peal of Bells* Robert Lynd; *Report from a Chinese Village* Jan Myrdal (Picador 1963); *The Prophet* Kahlil Gibran; *Mama Dot's Treatise* Fred D'Aguiar (Chatto 1985); *Long Walk to Freedom* Nelson Mandela (Abacus 1995); *My Mother the Land* Rrurrambu Dhurrkay; *The Warriors of the Rainbow, The Silent Spring* Rachel Carson (Houghton Mifflin 1962); *The Imperial Animal* Lionel Tiger and Robin Fox (1971); *Tools for Conviviality* Ivan Illich (1973); *The Woman from Aleduma* Aline França (Clarindo Silva 1981); *Testimonies of Exile* Abena PA Busia (Africa World Press 1990); *Talking Back:Thinking Feminist - Thinking Black* bell hooks (South End Press 1989); *The Mask of Anarchy* PB Shelley; *Confirmation* Gayl Jones (Morrow 1983); *The Future and the Ancestor* Andrée Chedid.

About
New Internationalist
Publications

New Internationalist is a publications co-operative
based in Oxford, UK, with editorial and sales offices in
Aotearoa/New Zealand, Australia and Canada.
It publishes the *New Internationalist* magazine on global issues,
which has 65,000 subscribers worldwide. The NI also produces
the One World Calendar, Almanac and Greetings Cards,
as well as publications such as *Eye to Eye: Women*
and food books including *The Spices of Life.*

For more information write to:

Aotearoa/New Zealand
PO Box 1905, Christchurch.

Australia and PNG
7 Hutt Street, Adelaide 5000,
South Australia.

Canada and US
35 Riviera Drive, Unit 17, Markham,
Ontario L3R 8N4.

United Kingdom
55 Rectory Road, Oxford OX4 1BW.

Contents

Introduction

It was almost a year ago that an ad appeared on the Letters Pages of the **New Internationalist** magazine saying that we were producing a book of quotes, and inviting readers to send in their favourites. The response was tremendous: phrases and sayings, proverbs and *bons mots* appeared in the mail on scraps of paper torn from notebooks; some had been carefully copied out; one or two came with a handwritten scrawl 'This is my favourite'; still others arrived by fax and phone, while several winged it over the Web.

What struck us as we sorted through this bounty was how people seem to love the ring of an idea, caught in a few words. They gather and store quotes like gems simply because they like the turn of a phrase, the way they feel the words speak to them and their situation - or because they feel a warmth or a sadness that links them with the person who spoke or wrote the words. Time and geography cannot create obstacles to this process. Or can it simply be that certain things don't change? 'Lying is the prerogative of the government' was Plato's view 2,300 years ago. No doubt you need some kind of conceit to be an authoritarian leader, and sure enough we find grandiose rubbish from Stalin, Hitler, Mussolini and Margaret Thatcher. Viewed from a safe distance their statements cause a smile or maybe grimace but take care, they meant every word... In this book, they are mostly confined to the section appropriately called 'Forked Tongue'.

It doesn't take much guesswork to see that this **NI** collection of quotes is quirky and subversive as well as sensitive and cynical. From the well of good sense that lies in most people - 'ordinary' women and men as well as writers, artists, poets and philosophers - we draw on thoughts about the environment, about love and friendship, about life, work, wealth and freedom. The book omits some of the traditional big guns of the quotes world - Shakespeare, for instance. But there are plenty of household names all the same: Oscar Wilde, Yoko Ono, Martin Luther King, Rebecca West, James Baldwin - people who have been at the sharp end of prejudice or spoken out for others. Well-known people from the South, such as Gandhi and author Bessie Head also find a place as well as many less familiar people whose words carry universal thoughts over barriers of race, culture and distance.

While most of the offerings are from broadly liberal people, non-sexist in outlook, the language is sometimes male-gendered. Where it was possible to change the words without killing the quote then this was done - 'mankind' into 'humanity' and 'men' into 'people' for example. But on some occasions the male language is entirely appropriate and so was left, as in Nez Percé Native American Chief Joseph's words: '*The white men were many and we could not hold our own with them. We were like deer. They were like grizzly bears.*'

People enjoy leafing through books of quotations for different reasons. Often it is to find one that they only partly remember. Sometimes it is just to wander along and bump into something new and interesting, revelatory perhaps or even funny. Others are seeking a motif or starting point for a talk and it's impressive how many books on public speaking suggest that the speaker use a quote either at the beginning or end of the speech (never both!). So although this isn't a speech, a quote is a good way to end. But which one? Should it be a big-name author, or somebody universally respected like Nelson Mandela? Perhaps an 'Anon' will do instead. How about: '*It is not what life does to you that is important, but what you do with what life does to you.*'?

Political punch
POWER AND POLITICS

The veto is an insidious tool,
to subvert democratic rule.
Samuel Oak Chilliwack, Canadian writer

The great difficulty with politics is that
there are no established principles.
Napoleon Bonaparte (1769-1821) French emperor

Do not put your faith in what statistics
say until you have carefully considered
what they do not say.
William W Watt

Politics is not the art of the possible.
It consists of choosing between the
disastrous and the unpalatable.
JK Galbraith (1908-) Canadian-born economist

There is no greater power on earth
than an idea whose time has come.
Victor Hugo (1802-1885) French writer

It is a great shock at the age of five
or six to find that in a world of Gary
Coopers you are the Indian.
James Baldwin (1924-1987) US writer

I am Black.
Okay?
Hot sun and the geographical set-up
Made me Black.
Bessie Head (1937-1986) South African-born writer

The white men were many and we could
not hold our own with them. We were
like deer. They were like grizzly bears.
Chief Joseph of the Nez Percé Native Americans, on
his decision to move out of the Wallowa valley in
Oregon to the Lapwai Reservation in Idaho, 1877

Official Latin American history boils down to a military parade of bigwigs in uniforms fresh from the dry-cleaners.

EDUARDO GALEANO (1940 –)
Uruguayan writer

3

Political punch

POWER AND POLITICS

History will absolve me.
Fidel Castro (1926-) Cuban leader, in the title of a 1953 pamphlet

The pursuit of power leads to isolation,
The death of human values and the death of the soul.
Anon

Race continues to mean now one thing, now another, because it has no meaning in itself.
Dinyar Godrej, in the New Internationalist

Only the law can rule on the law.
New Zealand/Aotearoa Maori saying

Never give up on what you really want to do - the person with big dreams is more powerful than one with all the facts.
Anon

The people, in any human corporate sense, do not determine any policies outside their backyards. The world is governed by the representatives of industry, finance, technology and by bureaucracies in the paid service of these powerful groups - governed, not in the interests of the people as a whole, not even of all the people in any one country, and not even nowadays for personal profit, but primarily for the self-satisfying exercise of power.
Sir Herbert Read (1893-1968) British poet and critic

Lying is the prerogative of the Government.
Plato (429-347 BC) Greek philosopher

Praise the Lord and pass the ammunition!

Howell Maurice Forgy (1908-) US naval lieutenant, remark made during 1941 Japanese attack on Pearl Harbour

You can fool all of the people some of the time, and some of the people all of the time. But you cannot fool all of the people all of the time.

Abraham Lincoln (1809-1865) US president

The myth of unlimited production brings war in its train as inevitably as clouds announce a storm.

Albert Camus (1913-1960) French existentialist writer

Washing one's hands of the conflict between the powerful and the powerless means to side with the powerful, not to be neutral.

Paulo Freire, contemporary Brazilian educationist

There are three kinds of lies: lies, damned lies and statistics.

Benjamin Disraeli (1804-1882) British prime minister

We can live without a president, but we can't live without farmers.

Placard by South Korean students protesting against President Kim Young Sam's decision to open the country's rice market to world trade

If you were to hold America on its side and shake it, everything that was loose would slide to California.

Lyndon B Johnson (1908-1973) US president

Political punch

POWER AND POLITICS

Nobody made a greater mistake than he who did nothing because he could do only a little.

Edmund Burke (1729-1797) British political thinker

Politics is the art of acquiring, holding and wielding power.

Indira Gandhi (1917-1984) Indian prime minister

When the white men came we had the land and they had the Bible. They taught us to pray with our eyes closed and when we opened them, they had the land and we had the Bible.

Jomo Kenyatta (1895-1978) president of Kenya

Poverty is not a fact of life but a result of sin by the powerful and therefore a cause of God's wrath.

Gustavo Gutierrez, contemporary Peruvian liberation theologist

Poor countries enjoy two basic rights: to sell cheap and buy dear.

Julius Nyerere (1922-) first president of Tanzania

The State represents violence in a concentrated and organised form. The individual has a soul, but as the State is a soulless machine, it can never be weaned from violence, to which it owes its very existence.

Mohandas K Gandhi (1869-1948) Indian nationalist leader

There is no birthright in the white skin that it shall say that wherever it goes, to any nation, amongst any people, there the people of the country shall give way before it, and those to whom the land belongs shall bow down and become its servants.
Annie Besant (1847-1933) British theosophist and political campaigner

The man who strikes first admits that his ideas have given out.
Chinese proverb

No ruling class in the whole of history has given up power voluntarily and I don't see that changing.
Tariq Ali, student activist and writer

For the inhabitants a great empire is nothing more than an excuse for vices and crimes which congregate in large cities as in a great sink into which the universe empties. For vice does not follow poverty nor misery but riches and power.
Juan Luis Vives (1492-1540)

As the twig is bent, the tree inclines.
Virgil (70-19 BC) Roman poet

The most potent weapon in the hands of the oppressor is the mind of the oppressed.
Steve Biko (1946-1977) South African Black Consciousness leader

Political punch
POWER AND POLITICS

When I look back, I see there is no way we could have regained our land, no way for our children to have got an education, if there hadn't been a 'Mau Mau'.

Former member of the 1950s Mau Mau rebellion in Kenya against British colonialism

Official Latin American history boils down to a military parade of bigwigs in uniforms fresh from the dry-cleaners.

Eduardo Galeano (1940-) Uruguayan writer

You loot, I shoot.

Bumper sticker in El Salvador

Grub first, then ethics.

Bertolt Brecht (1896-1956) German playwright

Nigerians do not normally ask questions about anything. Things just happen. So a bloke just strolls to the radio station and says 'Hello, I'm now your new Head of State'. And the Nigerians take to the street, dancing.

Ken Saro-Wiwa (1941-1995) executed Nigerian writer and activist

If everybody in the world says they want peace, how can we still sell guns? Somebody must be lying.

Joan Brooklyn, US, aged 10

This is the fire that will help the generations to come, if they use it in a sacred manner. But if they do not use it well, the fire will have the power to do them great harm.
Sioux Native American saying

An end requiring unjust means is not a just end.
Karl Marx (1818-1883) German philosopher and revolutionary

Sovereignty was wrested from us as a people. Equally undeniable however is the fact that with the act of recovering sovereignty... African leadership did not give much thought to the justice of reinvesting that sovereignty in its people.
General Ibrahim Babangida, president of Nigeria 1985-1993

Why are stamps adorned with kings and presidents? That we may lick their hinder parts and thump their heads.
Howard Nemerov (1920-1991) US poet

It is better to believe in people than in states. At moments of serious doubt you have to cling to the reality of people.
Wole Soyinka (1934-) Nigerian writer and Nobel Prizewinner for literature

Some white people are so accustomed to operating at a competitive advantage that when the playing field is level, they feel handicapped.
Nathan McCall, contemporary US writer

Political punch
POWER AND POLITICS

I think we must save America from the missionary idea that you must get the whole world on to the American way of life. This is really a big world danger.
Gunnar Myrdal (1898-1987) Swedish economist and Nobel Peace Prizewinner

Bad officials are elected by good citizens who do not vote.
George J Nathan (1882-1958) US critic

The death of democracy is not likely to be an assassination by ambush. It will be a slow extinction from apathy, indifference and undernourishment.
Robert M Hutchins (1899-1977) US educator

The society of money and exploitation has never been charged, so far as I know, with assuring the triumph of freedom and justice.
Albert Camus (1913-1960) French existentialist writer

It is accepted that every form of pride, every form of vanity, and even the most stupid boastings are legitimate and honourable so long as they are attributed to the nation in which one has taken the trouble to get born...
Denis de Rougemont

Under capitalism man exploits man; under socialism the reverse is true.
Polish proverb

If I had not been born Perón, I would have liked to be Perón.
Juan Perón (1895-1974) Argentinian president

The youth of today and those to come after them would assess the work of the revolution in accordance with values of their own... a thousand years from now, all of them even Marx, Engels and Lenin, would possibly appear rather ridiculous.
Mao Zedong (1893-1976) Chinese leader

I'd much rather have that fellow inside my tent pissing out, than outside my tent pissing in.
Lyndon B Johnson (1908-1973) US president, when asked why he kept J Edgar Hoover as director of the FB1

I am responsible only to God and history.
Generalissimo Francisco Franco (1892-1975) Spanish nationalist leader

The law doth punish the man or woman That steals the goose from off the common. But lets the greater felon loose That steals the common from the goose.
Anon 18th century epigram

Violence is the last refuge of the incompetent.
Isaac Asimov (1920-) US writer

You cannot shake hands with a clenched fist.
Indira Gandhi (1917-1984) Indian prime minister

I never dared be radical when young For fear it would make me conservative when old.
Robert Frost (1874-1963) US poet

Political punch
POWER AND POLITICS

A conservative is a man who just sits and thinks, mostly sits.
Woodrow Wilson (1856-1924) US president

We know what happens to people who stay in the middle of the road - they get run over.
Aneurin Bevin (1897-1960) British politician

Conservatives are not necessarily stupid, but most stupid people are conservative.
John Stuart Mill (1806-1873) British philosopher

Democracy is good. I say this because other systems are worse.
Jawaharlal Nehru (1889-1964) first prime minister of India

Men who have greatness within them don't go in for politics.
Albert Camus (1913-1960) French existentialist writer

There can be no daily democracy without daily citizenship.
Ralph Nader (1934-) US consumer lawyer and activist

A dictatorship is a country where they have taken the politics out of politics.
Sam Himmell, US politician

A society of sheep must in time beget a government of wolves.
Bertrand de Jouvenel

If there be one... doctrine more contrary to truth than any other, it is the notion that individual interest... is a more advantageous principle on which to found the social system... than the principle of union and mutual cooperation.
Robert Owen (1771-1858) British socialist thinker

Political punch
POWER AND POLITICS

An empty stomach is not a good political adviser.
Albert Einstein (1879-1955) German-born physicist

No amount of political freedom will satisfy the hungry masses.
VI Lenin (1870-1924) Russian revolutionary leader

He who lives by the sword shall perish by the champagne cocktail.
Saul Alinsky (1909-1972) US radical

All cruelty springs from weakness.
Seneca (4 BC-65 AD) Roman writer

A government is the only known vessel that leaks from the top.
James Reston (1909-) US political commentator

Those who persuade themselves that the masses of men distracted by politics can ever be induced to live according to the bare dictate of reason must be dreaming of the poetic golden age or of a stage play.
Baruch de Spinoza (1632-1677) Dutch philosopher

Nothing is so admirable in politics as a short memory.
JK Galbraith (1908-) Canadian-born economist

Find out what Bill Gates [of Microsoft] wants your school to do. Don't do it.
Theodore Roszak (1933-) US cultural thinker and writer, on computers and education

If you think you're too small to be effective you've obviously never been in bed with a mosquito.
Anon

Life lines
LIFE AND EXPERIENCE

What is life? It is the flash of a firefly in the night. It is the breath of a buffalo in the winter time. It is the little shadow which runs across the grass and loses itself in the sunset.

Chief Crowfoot of the Blackfoot Native Americans, in his dying hours, 1890

One never notices what has been done; one can only see what remains to be done.

Marie Curie (1867-1934) Polish-born chemist

A journey of a thousand miles begins with a single step.

Chinese proverb

All events in your life are there because you are drawn to them, what you choose to do with them is up to you.

Richard Bach, US writer

There is a magic formula for resolving conflicts. It is this:
Have as your objective the resolving of the conflict, not the gaining of advantage.

Peace Pilgrim

I see that a plant grows in a place where it can be strong and good. If I pull it up and carry it to some other place it may not grow well.

The Akawaio Indians of Guyana, referring to their removal to make way for a hydro-electric scheme

There are only two worries in this world:
The worry that you can resolve - so do something about it!
The worry that you can't resolve - so forget about it...

Mike Harper

The trouble with the rat race is that even if you win, you're still a rat.

LILY TOMLIN (1936–) US ACTRESS

Life lines
LIFE AND EXPERIENCE

If we were supposed to talk more than we listen, we would have two mouths and one ear.
Mark Twain (1835-1910) US writer

The value of life lies not in the length of days, but in the use we make of them.
Anon

When the forms of an old culture are dying, the new culture is created by a few people who are not afraid to be insecure.
Rudolf Bahro, member of the German Green Party

Let us put our minds together and see what life we can make for our children.
Sitting Bull (c1834-1890) Sioux Native American chief

If you plan for a year, plant rice.
If you plan for ten years, plant trees.
If you plan for one hundred years,
  educate your children.
Chinese proverb

The important thing is that [every] day should be useful, should be meaningful!
Dalai Lama (1935-) Tibetan spiritual leader

I have six honest serving men.
They taught me all I know.
Their names are What and Why and When
And How and Where and Who.
Rudyard Kipling (1865-1936) British writer

This is my home. Look how wonderful it is! Look what we have done! Look what we have made here! Isn't it beautiful? Don't you think so? Sit down! Eat! Have breakfast! Have lunch! Eat what we have made! Welcome!
Pamela Cahuana Flores, Peruvian coffee producer, welcoming a visitor from overseas

If you are doing something, and you meet difficulties, and this makes you more interested in that thing, then that is what you should be in life.
Rene Telek

There's one thing about musicians. They're all temperamental bastards. There's one thing about record companies, they don't know how to be temperamental, they're just bastards.
The Ruthless Rap Assassins

I hope you come to find that which gives life a deep meaning for you. Something worth living for - maybe even worth dying for. Something that energizes you, enthuses you, enables you to keep moving ahead.

I can't tell you what it might be - that's for you to find, to choose, to love. I can just encourage you to start looking, and support you in the search.
Written by **Sister Ita Ford** to her niece, shortly before Ford was murdered in the civil war in El Salvador, December 2 1980

The best [development] projects don't involve outsiders at all, but to say so is seen as a blasphemy against 'development'.
Pandurang Hegde, Indian environmental activist

17

Life lines
LIFE AND EXPERIENCE

Once you start a person thinking there is no telling where they will go...
Paulo Freire, contemporary Brazilian educationist

Sometimes I wish I were like a taxi driver in Lagos, who at the end of the day just wants a cold beer.
Olisa Agbakoba, Nigerian human-rights lawyer

The reasonable adapt themselves to the world; the unreasonable adapt the world to themselves. Therefore all progress depends on those who are unreasonable.
George Bernard Shaw (1856-1950) Irish dramatist and critic

What is terrible when you seek the truth is that you find it. You find it and you are no longer free to follow the biases of your personal circle, or to accept fashionable clichés.
Victor Serge (1890-1947) Russian-born writer and activist

I want to earn my own living and live my own life, with a home of my own. I don't want someone else to have control of me.
Gohar Kordi, contemporary Iranian writer

Yesterday is but tomorrow's memory and tomorrow is today's dream.
Kahlil Gibran (1883-1931) Lebanese poet

We are not living in a museum here. We welcome change. Our culture, our traditions are strong and alive because they adapt, they change.
Antonio, a Huichol indian leader in Mexico, 1994

Our lives are inextricably linked by the common thread of humanity. If we break it, we are all undone.
Peter Adamson, contemporary writer on development

You don't need a Weatherman
To know which way the wind blows.
Bob Dylan (1941-) US musician

My life is hard; I work all day in the cane fields. What good would it do to lie awake crying about my fate? Can I argue with God for the state I'm in? No! So I'll dance and I'll jump and I'll play *carnaval*! Yes, I'll laugh and people will wonder at a poor person like me who can have such a good time... but if I don't enjoy myself a little bit, well then I would rather be dead.
Biu, a woman from Northeast Brazil, 1994

Enjoy life - this is not a dress rehearsal.
Anon

Right now you are the latest edition.
Tai Situpa, Tibetan Lama

If you find something good, share it with anyone you can find. In that way the goodness will spread, no telling how far it will go.
Forest Carter, contemporary US writer

The trouble with the rat-race is that even if you win, you're still a rat.
Lily Tomlin (1936-) US actress

Life lines
LIFE AND EXPERIENCE

It is a law of human life, as certain as gravity: to live fully, we must learn to use things and love people... not love things and use people.
Anon

You can close your eyes to reality but not to memories.
Stanislaus Lec (1909-1966) Polish poet

Defoe [the writer] says that there were a hundred thousand country fellows in his time ready to fight to the death against popery without knowing whether popery was a man or a horse.
William Hazlitt (1778-1830) British writer and critic

In the stream where you least expect it, you'll find fish.
Chinese saying

Show the light and the people will find the way.
Motto of the West African *Pilot* newspaper in Nigeria, founded by the country's first president, Nnamdi Azikiwe (1904-1996)

Life is walking fast
It wasn't how I wanted it, but I had to take what I could.
Véronique Tadjo (1955-) writer from Côte d'Ivoire

It happened that a fire broke out backstage in a theatre. A clown came out to inform the public about it. They thought it was a joke and applauded. He repeated it; people laughed even more. This is the way I think the world will end - with general giggling by all the witty heads, who think it is a joke.
Søren Kierkegaard (1813-1855) Danish philosopher

People's progress is nothing but the victory of laughter over dogma.
Anon

We must pass
through solitude and
difficulty, isolation and silence
to find that enchanted place where
we can dance our clumsy dance and sing our
sorrowful song. But in that dance, and in
that song, the most ancient rites of our
conscience fulfil themselves
in the awareness of
being human.
Pablo Neruda (1904-1973) Chilean poet

It is not what life does to you that is important but what you do with what life does to you.
Chinese saying

Everyone seems to have hernias now.
Darren Anderton (1972-) Tottenham and England footballer, on his return to the squad after a hernia operation

If I thought the world were to end tomorrow, I would still plant an apple tree today.
Martin Luther King (1929-1968) US civil rights leader

In the beginner's mind there are many possibilities; in the expert's mind there are few.
Shunryu Suzuki, Zen philosopher

Those who live in a palace do not think about the same things, nor in the same way, as those who live in a hut.
Thomas Sankara (1949-1987) president of Burkina Faso

Life lines
LIFE AND EXPERIENCE

The condition of alienation, of being asleep... unconscious... out of one's mind, is the condition of the normal man. Society highly values its normal man. It educates children to lose themselves and to become absurd, and thus to be normal. Normal men have killed perhaps 100,000,000 of their fellow normal men in the last fifty years... It is quite certain that unless we can regulate our behaviour much more satisfactorily than at present... we are going to exterminate ourselves.
RD Laing (1927-1989) British psychiatrist

If you haven't been happy very young, you can still be happy later on, but it's much harder. You need more luck.
Simone de Beauvoir (1908-1986) French philosopher and writer

I shall repent, but not yet.
St Augustine (340-430)

We are here today and gone tomorrow.
Aphra Benn (1640-1689) British writer

People are about as happy as they decide that they are going to be.
Abraham Lincoln (1809-1865) US president

He no play-a-da game. He no make-a-da rules!
Earl Butz (1909-   ) US politician, on the Pope's stance on contraception

You don't get to choose how you're going to die. Or when. You can only decide how you're going to live. Now.
Joan Baez (1941-   ) US folksinger and civil rights activist

They fuck you up, your mum and dad.
They may not mean to, but they do.
They fill you with the faults they had
And add some extra, just for you.
Philip Larkin (1922-85) British poet

Tolerance is the oil which takes the friction out of life.
Anon

Do not be sad that you have suffered;
be glad that you have lived.
Joan Anglund, poet

The only thing we have to fear is fear itself.
Franklin D Roosevelt (1882-1945) US president

I've never had problems
with drugs, only with police.
Keith Richards (1943-)
Rolling Stones guitarist

Suffer fools gladly; they may be right.
Holbrook Jackson (1874-1948) British writer

In a war of ideas it is people who get killed.
Stanislaus Lec (1909-1966) Polish poet

The ways of your ancestors are good
They cannot be blown away by the winds
Because their roots reach deep into
the soil.
Okot p'Bitek, Ugandan poet

Life lines
LIFE AND EXPERIENCE

Truth has been eaten by the pigs.
Russian peasant saying

Give a person a fish, you feed them for a day. Teach them to fish, you feed them for life.
Chinese proverb

Only two things will come through the nuclear holocaust: the cockroach and the Calcuttan - and not necessarily in that order.
Joke told by Calcuttans

One cannot build life from refrigerators, politics, credit statements and crossword puzzles. That is impossible. Nor can one exist for any length of time without poetry, without colour, without love.
Antoine de Saint-Exupéry (1900-1944) French writer

Music is your own experience, your thoughts, your wisdom. If you don't live it, it won't come out of your horn.
Charlie Parker (1920-1955) US saxophonist

Be eccentric - society needs you.
Anon

I want the culture of all lands to be blown about my house as freely as possible.
Mohandas K Gandhi (1869-1948) Indian nationalist leader

Solitude shows us what we should be; society shows us what we are.
Lord David Cecil (1902-1986) British writer and critic

I keep my eyes on the moon and my feet muddy.
Anon

We are what we do.
Eric Fromm (1900-1980) US philosopher and writer

Job endured everything - until his friends came to comfort him. Then he grew impatient.
Søren Kierkegaard (1813-1855) Danish philosopher

We need to counter the dehumanising images of old age with new ones that enable us to be comfortable with our bodies. We need to continue to grow, learn and keep our minds and spirits vibrant as long as we live.
Maggie Kuhn, founder of the Grey Panthers organization for older people

It is not the quality of the food, but the cheerfulness of the guests which makes the feast.
Anon

If we ourselves remain always angry and then sing world peace, it has little meaning. So first our individual self must learn peace. This we can practice. Then we can teach the rest of the world.
Dalai Lama (1935-) Tibetan spiritual leader

Each generation has a different language, and can't learn what former generations knew, until it has been translated into their words.
Katherine Butler Hathaway

Lay plans for the accomplishment of the difficult before it becomes difficult; make something big by starting with it when small.
Lao Tzu, 6th century BC Chinese philosopher

Life lines
LIFE AND EXPERIENCE

If you weep once you weep forever.
Vietnamese saying

The great thing about getting older is that you don't lose all the other ages you've been.
Madelaine L'Engle

Existence should be met on its own terms: we may dance around with it, and perhaps steal a kiss; but it tempts us only to flout us, not being dedicated to any constant love...
George Santayana (1863-1952) US philosopher

The path to your heart's desire is never overgrown.
Kigezi proverb, Uganda

Here's a riddle for our age: when the sky's the limit, how can you tell when you've gone too far?
Rita Dove (1952-) US poet

I accept myself, and accept that life does not have to be long to be beautiful. I tried to swim and nearly drowned. My lungs caught fire, but the fire became a lamp light to the stars. My body grew light and free and a pure, clean water washed away my fear and made me whole. Now I swim towards a new life and I am no longer afraid. Swim with me.
Olivia Havyatt, young Australian cancer sufferer

The best of all true things is a true heart. Without truth, no happiness, though you try a million tricks.
Kabir, 15th century Indian poet

Only one of me
and nobody can get a second one
from a photocopy machine.
James Berry (1924-) Jamaican poet

Football isn't a matter of life or death.
It is much more important than that.
Bill Shankly (1914-1981) former manager of Liverpool
Football Club, UK

Because I came to know strength
I can praise tenderness.
Rainer Maria Rilke (1875-1926) Austrian poet

Smiles have one thing in common -
they are all different.
Anon

I don't sing a song unless I feel it. The
song don't tug at my heart, I pass on it.
I have to believe in what I'm doing.
Ray Charles (1930-) US pianist and singer

An ugly thing, that is what you are
when you become a tourist, an ugly,
empty thing, a stupid thing, a piece of
rubbish pausing here and there to gaze
at this and taste that, and it will never
occur to you that the people who
inhabit the place in which you have just
paused cannot stand you.
Jamaica Kincaid (1949-) Antiguan writer

Take time to be happy. Time
is not a fast lane between
cradle and grave. It is a place
to park out of the sun.
Anon

Life is what happens to you when
you're busy making other plans.
Indian saying

Life lines
LIFE AND EXPERIENCE

People must choose whether to be rich in things or in the freedom to use them.
Ivan Illich (1926-) US sociologist

Whatever you can do
Or dream you can do, begin it.
Boldness has genius, power and magic in it.
Begin it now.
Johann W von Goethe (1749-1832) German writer

If you can't count, they can cheat you.
If you can't read, they can beat you.
Toni Morrison (1931-) US writer

Violence is as American as cherry pie.
H Rap Brown (Jamil Abdullah Al-Amin)

The struggle is my life.
Nelson Mandela (1918-) first black president of South Africa, in 1961

If you know you're alive, find the essence of life.
Life is the sort of guest you don't meet twice.
Kabir, 15th century Indian poet

The medium is the message.
Marshall McLuhan (1911-1981) Canadian sociologist

When you see a snake, never mind where it came from.
WG Benham, US writer

A child who is to be successful is not reared exclusively on a bed of down.
Akan proverb, Ghana

Life lines
LIFE AND EXPERIENCE

The unfortunate thing about this world is that good habits are so much easier to give up than bad ones.

W Somerset Maugham (1874-1965) British writer

Experience enables you to recognize a mistake when you make it again.

Franklin Jones (1939-) US spritual thinker

All poor people ain't black and All black people ain't poor.

African-American saying

Live simply that others may simply live.

Mohandas K Gandhi (1869-1948) Indian nationalist leader

Forgiveness is the key to action and freedom.

Hannah Arendt (1906-1975) US philosopher

I have developed the habit of not having any habits.

Khalida Messaoudi, Algerian feminist under threat of assassination

I have found the best way to give advice to your children is to find out what they want and then advise them to do it.

Harry S Truman (1884-1972) US president

We have been recipients of assistance from all over the world... We are now in a position not only to do things for ourselves - we must assist others as well.

Kgalema Motlanthe, general secretary, National Union of Mineworkers, South Africa

Life lines
LIFE AND EXPERIENCE

Almost everything that you do will be insignificant, but it is very important that you do it.
Mohandas K Gandhi (1869-1948) Indian nationalist leader

To avoid criticism, don't do anything, say anything or be anything.
Anon

Whoever wants to be admired at a festival should be prepared to dance well.
Igbo proverb, Nigeria

Treat your guest as a guest for two days; on the third day, give them a hoe!
Swahili saying

The best substitute for experience is being sixteen.
Raymond Duncan

Many of the things we need can wait. The child cannot.
Gabriela Mistral (1889-1957) Chilean poet and politician

Children have never been very good at listening to their elders, but they have never failed to imitate them.
James Baldwin (1924-1989) US writer

I'd rather have a bottle in front of me that a frontal lobotomy.
Tom Waites, contemporary US musician

Only the shallow know themselves.
Oscar Wilde (1854-1900) Irish-born dramatist

If you speak, speak to her who understands you.
Senegalese proverb

Data, data everywhere
And not a thought to think.
Anon

We are surer that we see a star when we know that others also see it.
Henry George

Travellers may tell what they have seen on their journey, but they cannot explain it all.
Ashanti saying, Ghana

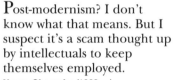

Post-modernism? I don't know what that means. But I suspect it's a scam thought up by intellectuals to keep themselves employed.
Noam Chomsky (1928-   )
US academic and activist

Money doesn't talk–it swears
WEALTH AND RICHES

My shack is very tidy and it may even be better than some posh houses in my area.
Paulos Majola, newspaper vendor, Johannesburg, South Africa

For every dollar that US companies invest in Latin America, three dollars accrue to the US in income.
US Department of Commerce

Efficiency in the World Bank is to move the greatest amount of money with the least amount of thought.
Herman Daly, former Bank official

It is the fool whose own tomatoes are sold to him.
Akan proverb, Ghana

Whoever is capable of knowing when they have had enough will always be satisfied.
Lao Tzu, 6th century BC Chinese philosopher

If all the rich people in the world divided up their money among themselves there wouldn't be enough to go round.
Christina Stead (1902-1983) Australian writer

There are three kinds of people in the world. Those who can count, and those who can't.
Anon

From each according to their abilities, to each according to their needs.
Karl Marx (1818-1883) German philosopher and revolutionary

If you want to steal some money, don't rob a bank - open one.
Bertolt Brecht (1896-1956) German playwright

It would be nice if hospitals and schools had all the money they needed and the army had to hold jumble sales to buy guns.

PETRA KELLY (1947-1992) LEADER OF THE GERMAN GREENS

CHEAP

Money doesn't talk-it swears
WEALTH AND RICHES

The poor person's goat does not give birth, or if she does, she has a male kid.

Tanzanian saying suggesting not only the disadvantaged position that poor peasants' enterprises start from, but also the difficulties of sustaining them

The white man knows how to make everything, but he does not know how to distribute it.
Chief Sitting Bull (c1834-1890) Sioux Native American

They gave me star treatment because I was making a lot of money. But I was just as good when I was poor.
Bob Marley (1945-1981) Jamaican reggae singer

Property is theft.
Pierre Joseph Proudhon (1809-1865) French socialist

It would be nice if hospitals and schools had all the money they needed and the army had to hold jumble sales to buy guns.
Petra Kelly (1947-1992) leader of the German Green Party

He must have killed a lot of people to have made so much money.
Molière (1622-1673) French dramatist

Our land is more valuable than your money. It will last forever.
Blackfoot Native American chief, on being asked to sign a land treaty

We are rich in proportion to the things we can leave alone.
Henry David Thoreau (1817-1862) US writer

Business parrots the rhetoric of Free Enterprise, but the multinationals look to Government to buy their goods, prop up their prices, subsidise their inefficiencies, protect their monopolies, minimize their competition, guarantee their credit, cover their losses, and absorb their bankruptcies.
Marilyn French (1929-   ) US writer

The slimming of an elephant and the losses of a rich man are not noticeable.
Amharic saying, Ethiopia

Borrowing is for amateurs, stealing is for artists.
Steve Jobs, founder of Apple Corp

Personal wealth is no more than a badge of competence at getting someone else to pay your bills.
David Ransom, New Internationalist co-editor

The law, in its majestic equality, forbids the rich as well as the poor to sleep under bridges, to beg in the streets, and to steal bread.
Anatole France (1844-1924) French writer

Poverty is the symptom; slavery the disease. The extremes of riches and destitution follow inevitably upon the extremes of licence and bondage. The many are not enslaved because they are poor, they are poor because they are enslaved.
GDH Cole, British historian

Money doesn't talk–it swears
WEALTH AND RICHES

Poverty has a home in Africa - like a quiet second skin.
Bessie Head (1937-1986) South African-born writer

There is just more and more month left over at the end of my money.
Millor Fernandes, Brazilian humorist, in 1974 on the country's soaring inflation

By 1962, according to a UN audit, General Mobutu of Zaire had diverted enough money from foreign military-aid programmes to make himself a millionaire. In 1965 he became President. [In 1997, he still was.]
New Internationalist magazine

More important than giving to the poor is to stop taking from them.
Anon

Wealth is not the fruit of labour but the result of organised protected robbery.
Frantz Fanon (1925-1961) Martinique-born writer

Few women care to be laughed at and men not at all, except for large sums of money.
Alan Ayckbourn (1939-) British playwright

A friend in the market-place is better than money in the chest.
West African proverb

Send me some of it [gold], because I and my companions suffer from a disease of the heart which can be cured only with gold.
Hernando Cortes, on seeing the Aztec gold, to King Montezuma in 1519

Money doesn't talk—it swears
WEALTH AND RICHES

Everyone wants to make money out of the Amazon....We live there and we are scared.
Paulinho Paiakan, Kayapo Indian leader

Rich men's houses are seldom beautiful, rarely comfortable and never original. It is a constant source of surprise to people of moderate means to observe how little a big fortune contributes to Beauty.
Margot Asquith (1865-1945) British socialite

To make the rich work harder you pay them more. To make the poor work harder you pay them less.
Anon

It's a kind of spiritual snobbery that makes people think they can be happy without money.
Albert Camus (1913-1960) French existentialist writer

Must we starve our children to pay our debts?
Julius Nyerere (1922-) first president of Tanzania, on the effects of structural adjustment programmes requiring cuts in public spending such as food subsidies

Of gold is treasure made, and with it he who has it does as he wills in the world and it even sends souls to paradise.
Christopher Columbus (1451-1506) Italian navigator

Money doesn't talk, it swears
Bob Dylan (1941-) US musician

Anyone who believes that exponential growth can go on for ever in a finite world is either mad or an economist.
Kenneth Boulding, contemporary economist

Money doesn't talk—it swears
WEALTH AND RICHES

When a man tells you that he got rich through hard work, ask him 'whose?'
Don Marquis (1878-1937) US journalist

The profits of our West Indian sugar are generally much greater than that from any other cultivation that is known.
Adam Smith (1723-1790) British economist

There is no people in the world so exhausted. I unburden my conscience to inform your Majesty... It is not silver that is brought to Spain, but the blood and sweat of Indians.
Count Lemos, Viceroy of Peru, in 1670 to the king of Spain

Man cannot live by profit alone.
James Baldwin (1924-1987) US writer

If you can enjoy a flower, a smile, the playing of a child, you are richer and happier than the richest, rich person.
Anon

When I give food to the poor they call me a saint. When I ask why the poor have no food they call me a communist.
Helder Camara, Archbishop of Recife, Brazil

Sown to be eaten, [corn] is the sacred sustenance of the people who were made of maize. Sown to make money, it means famine for the people who were made of maize.
Miguel Angel Asturias (1899-1974) Guatemalan Nobel Prizewinner for literature

Gentility is what's left over from rich ancestors after the money is gone.
John Ciardi (1916-1986) US writer

Business? It's quite simple. It's other people's money.
Alexandre Dumas (1824-1895) French writer

If the government was as afraid of disturbing the consumer as it is of disturbing business, this would be some democracy.
Frank McKinney Hubbard (1868-1930) US writer

There two times in life when you should not speculate: when you can't afford it and when you can.
Mark Twain (1835-1910) US writer

Capital as such is not evil; it is its wrong use that is evil.
Mohandas K Gandhi (1869-1948)
Indian nationalist leader

Poverty is the mother of crime.
Marcus Aurelius Antonius (121-180 AD) Roman emperor

Private enterprise... makes OK private action which would be considered dishonest in public action.
John F Kennedy (1917-1963) US president

Being there

REFLECTIONS ON LIFE

[The US] will never be a civilized country until we spend more money for books than we do for chewing gum.
Elbert Hubbard (1856-1915) US writer

The most profitable items on the Songhai [empire] market in the sixteenth century were books, because of the large demand.
From an introduction to the history of Mali

Any intelligent fool can make things bigger, more complex and more violent. It takes a touch of genius - and a lot of courage - to move in the opposite direction.
EF Schumacher (1911-1977) British economist

Experience is a good teacher, but she sends in terrific bills.
Minna Antrim (b 1861) US writer

Misunderstandings don't exist - only the failure to communicate.
Senegalese proverb

Don't compromise yourself You're all you've got.
Janis Joplin (1945-1970) US rock singer

To know what is right and not to do it is the worst cowardice.
Confucius (551-479 BC) Chinese philosopher

The best things in life aren't things.
Anon

No call alligator "long mouth" until you pass him.

US SLAVE SAYING

41

Being there
REFLECTIONS ON LIFE

There is a point beyond which forbearance ends and tolerance ceases to be a virtue.
Edmund Burke (1729-1797) British political thinker

Where is the life we have lost in living?
Where is the wisdom we have lost in knowledge?
Where is the knowledge we have lost in information?
TS Eliot (1888-1965) British writer

I know I'm not black, but there's some times I wish I could say I wasn't white either.
Frank Zappa (1940-) US rock singer

To me as a tribal Aboriginal, dreaming is more than just an ordinary dream which one would dream at night or day. To us, dreaming is reality because it takes in all the Aboriginal spirituality.
Djiniyini Gondarra, Australian aboriginal writer

The well-being of the world, its peace and security, are unattainable unless and until its unity is firmly established.
Bahá'u'lláh, founder of the Bahá'í faith, to Queen Victoria from the fortress of Akka in Palestine where he was a prisoner of the Turkish Sultan

What is success?
To laugh often and much;
To win the respect of intelligent people and the affection of children.
To earn the appreciation of honest critics and to endure the betrayal of false friends.
To appreciate beauty;
To find the best in others.
To leave the world a bit better whether by a healthy child, a garden patch or a redeemed social condition.
To know even one life has breathed easier because you have lived.
This is to have succeeded.
Ralph Waldo Emerson (1803-1882) US poet

Work on yourself first;
Take the responsibility for your
own progress.
I Ching

If we take a man as he is, we make him;
if we take him as he ought to be, we
help him to become it.
Johann W von Goethe (1749-1832) German poet

There is a destiny that makes us
brothers.
None goes the way alone,
All that we send into the lives of others
Comes back into our own.
Anon

God can only be seen when we sleep,
and his face has the features of those
who are closest to us.
Nawal el Sadaawi (b 1930s) Egyptian writer

I dislike dogmas and certainties. I delve
in ambiguity, in that reflective field
where reality appears at its most real.
Luisa Valenzuela (1938-) Argentinian writer

There is a light that shines beyond all
things on earth, beyond us all, beyond
the heavens, beyond the highest, the
very highest heavens. This is the light
that shines in our heart.
Chandogya Upanishad (Hindu scriptures)

The stone in the water
does not know how hot the
hill is, parched by the sun.
Nigerian proverb

Being there
REFLECTIONS ON LIFE

Cricket is a game which the English, not being a spiritual people, have invented in order to give themselves some conception of Eternity.
Lord Mancroft (1917-1987) British politician

Minds are like parachutes - they need to be fully open to operate properly.
Anon

I think somehow we learn who we really are and then live with that decision.
Eleanor Roosevelt (1884-1962) US writer and feminist

Everyone complains about their [own] memory, but none about their judgement.
François de la Rochefoucauld (1613-1680) French writer

One who knows much does not speak much.
Amharic saying, Ethiopia

Someone asked Gandhi: 'What do you think of civilisation in Britain?' Gandhi replied: 'I think it would be a very good idea.'

Patience is a bird that hatches great eggs.
Zulu saying

How I wish I could pigeon-hole myself and neatly fix a label on!
But self-knowledge comes too late and by the time I've known myself I am no longer what I was.
Mabel Segun (1930-) Nigerian writer

If relativity is proved right the Germans will call me a German, the Swiss will call me a Swiss citizen, and the French will call me a great scientist.
If relativity is proved wrong the French will call me a Swiss, the Swiss will call me a German, and the Germans will call me a Jew.
Albert Einstein (1879-1955) German-born physicist

Things which matter most must never be at the mercy of those [things] which matter least.
Johann W von Goethe (1749-1832) German writer

Nature teaches us by the sensations of hunger, thirst and so on, that I am not merely lodged in my body as a pilot in a ship but that I am very closely united and as it were intermingled with it.
René Descartes (1596-1650) French philosopher

We are distinguished from all other creatures by the faculty of laughter.
Joseph Addison (1672-1719) British writer

One retreat paves the way for another.
Anon

Who ask
don't get
Who don't ask
don't want
don't get
Who don't get
don't care.
Merle Hodge
(1944-)
Trinadadian writer

I thought that an inner heaven could make a heaven on earth.
Bessie Head (1937-1986) South African-born writer

45

Being there
REFLECTIONS ON LIFE

The water of the river goes fleeing from itself:
It is afraid of its eternity.
Dulce María Loynaz (1903-   ) Cuban poet

No one wants advice - only corroboration.
John Steinbeck (1902-1968) US writer

We are each the authors of our own lives.
We live in what we created.
There is no way to shift blame
And no-one else to accept the accolades.
Anon

Fifty lemons are a load for one person, but for fifty persons they are perfume.
Amharic saying, Ethiopia

If you can't invent a really convincing lie, it's often better to stick to the truth.
Angela Thirkell (1890-1961) British writer

We can easily forgive a child who is afraid of the dark; the real tragedy is when people are afraid of the light.
Plato (429-347 BC) Greek philosopher

When people agree with me I always feel I must be wrong.
Oscar Wilde (1854-1900) Irish-born writer

If Kitchener was not a great man, he was, at least, a great poster.
Margot Asquith (1864-1945) British socialite

Seven Deadly Sins
Politics without principle
Wealth without work
Commerce without morality
Pleasure without conscience
Education without character
Science without humanity
Worship without sacrifice.
Mohandas K Gandhi (1869-1948) Indian
nationalist leader

Give peace a chance.
John Lennon (1940-1980) British rock musician

If the stool says you farted - you farted!
**Wafipa saying from south-west Tanzania, used by a
chief when passing judgement in a paternity suit**

Justice is like a train that's nearly
always late.
Yevgeny Yevtushenko (1933-) Russian poet

For increase, it is beneficial to go
somewhere; it is beneficial to cross
great rivers.
I Ching

I am a lone monk walking the world with a
leaky umbrella.
Mao Zedong (1893-1976) Chinese leader

When we die, we die - the wind blows
away our footprints and that is the end
of us.
The San people of the Kalahari, southern Africa

To be is to do - Descartes
To do is to be - Jean-Paul Sartre
DoBeDoBeDo - Frank Sinatra
Graffiti

Being there
REFLECTIONS ON LIFE

There is that difference between being kicked in the teeth and reading a description of being kicked in the teeth - some call it existential.

Gita Mehta, contemporary Indian writer

Look not into the abyss lest the abyss look into you.

Friedrich Nietzsche (1844-1900) German philosopher

To live is to hope.

Cambodian proverb

If you attempt any of the Saharan tracks in Algeria... it is important to apply for a travel permit and give a precise route. This does not necessarily guarantee you will be rescued, but it makes it a possibility.

Guidebook

Human compassion is equal to human cruelty, and it is up to each of us to tip the balance.

Alice Walker (1944-) US writer

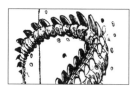

All of us lie in the gutter, but some of us are looking at the stars.

Oscar Wilde (1854-1900) Irish-born writer

In spite of everything, I still believe that people are really good at heart.

Anne Frank (1929-1945) Jewish diarist and victim of the Holocaust

Aboriginal achievement is like the dark side of the moon, it is there but so little is known.

Ernie Dingo, aboriginal Australian

Being there
REFLECTIONS ON LIFE

It is better to light one candle than curse the darkness.
Eleanor Roosevelt (1884-1962) US feminist and writer; also Peter Benenson, on the foundation of Amnesty International in 1961, from a Chinese saying

All of man's troubles stem from a single cause: his inability to sit quietly in a room.
Blaise Pascal (1623-1662) French writer

I hear and I forget. I see and I remember. I do and I understand.
Chinese proverb

It could be said that Brazil has its body in America and its soul in Africa.
Eduardo Galeano (1940-) Uruguayan writer

What comes from the lips reaches the ear. What comes from the heart, reaches the heart.
Arab proverb

The first camel in the train holds everyone up, but it is the last which gets the beating.
Amharic proverb, Ethiopia

Solitude, solitude so sought after... I love you
so much, that I'm sometimes afraid that God
will punish me some day by filling my life up with you...
Dulce María Loynaz (1903-) Cuban poet

When elephants fight the ants get trampled.
Malaysian saying

Being there
REFLECTIONS ON LIFE

Truth-tellers are not always palatable. There is a preference for candy bars.
Gwendolyn Brooks (1917-) US writer

When the mind becomes tranquil, then all things will be seen not in their separateness, but in their unity.
Surangama Sutra, Hindu religious treatise

Live in your beliefs and you can turn the world around.
Henry David Thoreau (1817-1862) US writer

With all beings and all things, we shall be as relatives.
Sioux Native American saying

Do not hurl a lance if you cannot aim correctly.
The Husia wisdom of ancient Egypt

After silence, that which comes nearest to expressing the inexpressible is music.
Aldous Huxley (1894-1963) British writer

The wise person looks into space, and does not regard the small as too little, nor the great as too big; for they know there is no limit to dimensions.
Lao-Tzu, 6th century BC Chinese philosopher

Many paths there be
To reach the mountain height.
But all who climb there see
The same moon's light.
Japanese author, 17th century

What hurts Indians most is that our costumes are considered beautiful but it's as if the person wearing it didn't exist.

Rigoberta Menchu, Guatemalan human rights activist and 1992 Nobel Peace Prizewinner

It's necessary for everything to stop for an instant before it ends.

Giannina Brashci (1954-) Puerto Rican poet

When it is dark enough you can see the stars.

Ralph Waldo Emerson (1803-1882) US poet

Bad as it is, the world is full of potentially good photographs. But to be good, photographs have to be full of the world.

Dorothea Lange (1895-1965) American photographer

Hope is ourselves – our children travelling towards a faith that feeds life.

Augustino Neto (1922-1979) poet and first president of Angola

Genius is childhood rediscovered at will.

Charles Baudelaire (1821-1867) French writer

...Till the morning comes my soul will light up the dark.

Afam Akeh, Nigerian poet

The road to ignorance is paved with good editions.

George Bernard Shaw (1856-1950) Irish writer

Being there
REFLECTIONS ON LIFE

Those who lose dreaming are lost.
Australian aboriginal proverb

It is generally believed that white men have quite the same minds as small children. They are easily angered, and when they cannot get their way, they are moody and, like children, have the strangest ideas and fancies.
Canadian Inuit, c1930

I am invisible, understand, simply because people refuse to see me.
Ralph Ellison (1914-) US writer

Blacks, having evidence to the contrary, still find it hard to accept the fact we really were the first to civilize the world.
Cheikh Anta Diop, Senegalese politician

A good name is better than perfume.
Amharic saying, Ethiopia

Your world is as big as you make it.
Anon

It ain't those parts of the Bible that I can't understand that bother me, it is the parts that I do understand.
Mark Twain (1835-1910) US writer

In America, black is a country.
Amiri Baraka

Being there
REFLECTIONS ON LIFE

A dream that you dream alone remains a dream
A dream that you share can become reality.
Anon

Only the fool points at his origins with his left hand.
Akan proverb, Ghana

A photograph is a secret about a secret. The more it tells you, the less you know.
Diane Arbus (1923-1971) American photographer

I do not believe in God, but I am afraid of him.
Gabriel Garcia Marquez, Colombian writer

In every work of genius we recognize our own rejected thoughts.
Ralph Waldo Emerson (1803-1882) US writer

There are three things I always forget. Names, faces - the third I can't remember.
Italo Svevo (1861-1928) Italian writer

It is all one to me if a man comes from Sing Sing [jail] or Harvard. We hire a man, not his history.
Henry Ford (1863-1947) US car manufacturer

Seeing ourselves as others see us would probably confirm our worst suspicions about them.
Franklin P Jones, contemporary US writer

Everything has been thought of before, but the problem is to think of it again.
Johann W von Goethe (1749-1832) German writer

Being there
REFLECTIONS ON LIFE

The world we have created today, as a result of our thinking thus far, has problems which cannot be solved by thinking the way we thought when we created them.
Albert Einstein (1879-1955) German-born physicist

Advertising is the rattling of a stick inside a swill bucket.
George Orwell (1903-1950) British writer

Don't talk unless you can improve the silence.
Chinese proverb

I have always thought of a dog lover as a dog that was in love with another dog.
James Thurber (1894-1961) US humorist

It is a far, far better thing to have a firm anchor in nonsense than to put out on the troubled seas of thought.
JK Galbraith (1908-) Canadian-born economist

When I am working on a problem, I never think about beauty. I think only how to solve the problem. But when I have finished, if the solution is not beautiful, I know it is wrong.
Buckminster Fuller (1895-1983) US architect

Civilization... is the acceptance and the encouragement of differences.
Mohandas K Gandhi (1869-1948) Indian nationalist leader

If the mind is dominated by hatred, the best part of the brain which is used to judge right and wrong does not function properly.
Dalai Lama (1935-) Tibetan spiritual leader

To read without reflecting is like eating without digesting.
Edmund Burke (1729-1797) British political thinker

Somebody's boring me... I think it's me.
Dylan Thomas (1914-1953) Welsh poet

It is a luxury to be understood.
Ralph Waldo Emerson (1803-1882) US poet

The only completely consistent people are the dead.
Aldous Huxley (1894-1964) British writer

You can live a lifetime and, at the end of it, know more about other people than about yourself. You learn to watch other people, but you never watch yourself because you strive against loneliness.
Beryl Markham (1902-1986) British-born aviator and writer

No call alligator long mouth until you pass him.
US slave saying

If England treats her criminals the way she has treated me, she doesn't deserve to have any.
Oscar Wilde (1854-1900) Irish-born writer

I was so long writing my review that I never got round to reading the book.
Groucho Marx (1890-1977) US actor

Criticism comes easier than craftmanship.
Zeuxis (400 BC)

Being there
REFLECTIONS ON LIFE

Don't ever slam a door; you might want to go back.
Anon

Generally the theories we believe we call facts, and the facts we disbelieve we call theories.
Felix Cohen

After ecstasy, there's laundry.
Zen thought

There is no failure except in no longer trying.
Elbert Hubbard (1856-1915) US writer

Don't catch a leopard by the tail, but if you do, don't let go.
Amharic proverb, Ethiopia

The writing on the wall may be a forgery.
Ralph Hodgson (1871-1962) US poet

When you dance the whole universe dances.
Jalaluddin Rumi (1207-1273) Afghani Sufi poet

A liar needs a good memory.
Quintilian (42-118) Roman orator

A fanatic is one who sticks to his guns whether they're loaded or not.
Franklin P Jones, contemporary US writer

It is by the goodness of God that in our country we have those three unspeakably precious things: freedom of speech, freedom of conscience and the prudence never to practice either of them.
Mark Twain (1835-1910) US writer

Everyone is a genius at least once a year; a real genius has their original ideas closer together.
GC Lichtenberg (1742-1799) German physicist and writer

I could prove God statistically.
George Gallup (1901-1984) US statistician and originator of Gallup public opinion polls

When choosing between two evils, I always like to try the one I've never tried before.
Mae West (1892-1980) US actress

Non-cooperation with evil is as much a duty as is cooperation with good.
Mohandas K Gandhi (1869-1948) Indian nationalist leader

The only thing necessary for the triumph of evil is for good people to do nothing.
Edmund Burke (1729-1797) British political thinker

Humour makes everything – and everyone – naked.
Hanan al-Shaykh, Lebanese novelist

If you're not allowed to laugh in heaven, I don't want to go there.
Martin Luther (1483-1546) German Protestant leader

Don't look back. Something may be gaining on you.
Leroy 'Satchel' Paige (1906-1982) US baseball player

Heroines

WOMEN

I'm not interested in struggling; I am interested in victory.
June Jordan (1936-) US poet

To the old saying that man built the house but woman made it a 'home' might be added the modern supplement that woman accepted cooking as a chore but man has made of it a recreation.
Emily Post (1873-1960) US writer

I am the washing machine
which the Señor won't buy
as long as I wash cheaper and
save the Señora
time
and her hands
rough skin
Caipora Women's Group, Brazil

The most important thing women have to do is to stir up the zeal of women themselves.
John Stuart Mill (1806-1873) British philosopher

Speak up for yourself, or you'll end up a rug.
Mae West (1892-1980) US actress

Sooner or later all men bark.
Octavia Saint Laurent, contemporary US writer

If men could become pregnant, abortion would be a sacrament.
Florynce R Kennedy (1916-) US lawyer and civil rights activist

Bad judgement and carelessness are not punishable by rape.
Pearl Cleage, contemporary US playwright

Heroines
WOMEN

You can't love someone unless you are in an equal position with them. A lot of women have to cling to men out of fear or insecurity, and that's not love. The problem for women is that if we try to be free, then we naturally become lonely, because so many women are willing to become slaves, and men usually prefer it.

Yoko Ono (1937-) artist and musician

I'm always interested to know how people who claim to be radical treat women.

John Lennon (1940-1980) British rock musician

Theres more poor than nonpoor theres more colored than noncolored theres more women than men.

Hattie Gossett (1942-) US writer

When poor men fight for wage increases or class revolution, their demands rarely include a doubling of their salary and a new method of payment, one that would reflect the importance of their wives' housework and childrearing. When poor men fight for wage increases it is to equalize some more power among men, and to allow more men to protect and own 'their' women and children in better ways.

Phyllis Chesler, contemporary US feminist and civil rights activist

Women are the survival kit of the human race.

Councillor Mandizvidza, Zimbabwe

The lesson we need to remember if we are to keep going with our cause [is that] serious opposition is a measure of success.

Gloria Steinem (1934-) US feminist writer

In the dust and strife of life in Parliament, I often longed for the peace and leisure of the days in purdah. But there could be no turning back, no returning to the secluded and sheltered existence of the past... I had to continue on this new road on which the women of my country had set out.

Shaista Ikramullah, Pakistani politician

In order to approach the highest job levels, women are expected to have more strengths and fewer faults than their male counterparts.

Ann M Morrison, Randall P White and **Ellen Van Velson**, authors of a report on workplace discrimination

So. The game was worth the candle. Was the candle worth the cake? Now you have it and you eat it Does it make your belly ache?

Jane King (1952-) St Lucian poet

In spite of everything we do, there's still the idea that women don't work, because they don't contribute economically to the home, that only the husband works because he gets a wage.

Domitila Barrios de Chungara, contemporary Bolivian activist

Heroines
WOMEN

Botany has lately become a fashionable amusement with the ladies. But how the study of the sexual systems of plants can accord with female modesty, I am not able to comprehend.

Richard Polwhele (1760-1838) British writer

I grew taller than my father
And my mother won.

Ishrat Aafreen, contemporary Pakistani poet

[A woman] is the first to work and last to rest. She is first to fetch water and wood, first at the fire, yet last to quench her thirst. She may eat only if there is food left and then only after the man. She is the very keystone of the family, carrying both family and society on her shoulders, in her hands, and in her belly.

Thomas Sankara (1949-1987) president of Burkina Faso

It is we sinful women
who are not awed by the grandeur of those who wear gowns
who don't sell our bodies
who don't bow our heads
who don't fold our hands together.

Kishwar Naheed, contemporary Pakistani poet

And God said: Adam,
What has thou done?
and Adam
With his head hung down,
Blamed it on the woman.

James Weldon Johnson (1871-1938)
US writer and civil rights advocate

The man is the peak of the house:
That is what we have understood.
It is women who make the pinnacle
On top of the roof.
Bemba saying, Zambia

Why should we pay taxes when we
have no part in the honours, the
commands, the statecraft, for which
you contend against each other with
such harmful results?
Hortensia (50 BC) Roman noblewoman and orator

I do not wish [women] to have power
over men; but over themselves.
Mary Wollstonecraft (1759-1797) British writer and
feminist

All I ask is the privilege for my
masculine part, the poet in me... if I
must not, because of my sex, have this
freedom, I lay down my quill and you
shall hear no more of me.
Aphra Benn (1640-1689) British writer

I do not ask for my rights.
I have no rights; I have only wrongs.
Caroline Norton (1808-1877) British
poet and campaigner for women's rights

If the first woman God made was strong
enough to turn the world upside down
all alone, these women together ought
to be able to turn it back, and get it
right side up again!
Sojourner Truth (c1797-1883) US slave
and abolitionist

Heroines
WOMEN

Even now, women bend to rivers
or to wells; they scoop up life and offer it
To men or to their children, to their elders,
To blistered cooking-pots.
Lucinda Roy (1956-) British writer

Housekeeping ain't no joke.
Louisa May Alcott (1832-88) US writer

The prolonged slavery of women is the
darkest page in human history.
Elizabeth Cady Stanton (1815-1902) US suffragette
and abolitionist

What a Woman may be, and yet not
have the Vote: mayor, nurse, mother,
doctor, teacher, factory hand.
What a Man may have been and yet not
lose the Vote: convict, lunatic,
proprietor of white slaves, unfit for
service, drunkard.
Poster used during British suffragette campaign
(c1901)

Women had always fought for men,
and for their children. Now they
were ready to fight for their own
human rights. Our militant
movement was established.
Emmeline Pankhurst (1858-1928) British
suffragette

Instead of this absurd division
into sexes they ought to class
people as static and dynamic.
Evelyn Waugh (1903-66) British novelist

If American politics are too dirty
for women to take part in, there's
something wrong with American politics.
Edna Ferber (1887-1968) US writer

According to civil law, women are equal to men. But I have to go to a religious court as far as personal affairs are concerned. Only men are allowed to be judges there - men who pray every morning to thank God He did not make them women.
Shulamit Aloni (1905-   ) Israeli lawyer, writing in 1973

Mothers raise their daughters and let their sons grow up.
African-American saying

People call me a feminist whenever I express sentiments that differentiate me from a doormat or a prostitute.
Rebecca West (1892-1893) British writer

She ascribed all the wrong in the world to male domination and narrowness, and would not see my experiences in the war as anything comparable with the sufferings that millions of working-class women went through without complaint.
Robert Graves (1895-1985) British writer

There are very few jobs that actually require a penis or a vagina. All other jobs should be open to everybody.
Florynce R Kennedy (1916-   ) US lawyer and civil rights activist

Heroines
WOMEN

Gradually the women of Egypt pulled down the silken curtain that separated them from the free world - the world of men. The voluntary removal of the veil by Egyptian women marked the beginning of a process of gradual emancipation.
Aziza Husain, Egyptian social reformer

Woman is born free and her rights are the same as those of a man...
Olympe de Gouges (1748-93) French writer and revolutionary, referring to the Declaration of the Rights of Man (1789)

I feel strongly that a rapist is a rapist, whether he is married to his victim or not.
John Patten (1945-) British politician

Now my heart turns to and fro, in thinking what will the people say. They who shall see my monument in after years, and shall speak of what I have done.
Hatsheput (1503-1482 BC) Egyptian queen, inscription on her obelisk

If women remain on the margins of the State, we only have marginal possibilities of making marginal change.
Rosa Maria Torres, director of literacy campaign, Ecuador

Why should marriage bring only tears?
All I wanted was a man
With a single heart,
And we would stay together
As our hair turned white,
Not somebody always after wriggling fish
With his big bamboo rod.
Chuo Wen-chun (c179-117 BC) Chinese poet

Love, struggle and work - the history of the world's women, past and future.
Rosalind Miles, contemporary British writer

My childhood was beautiful, beautiful, with hardworking hands. Full of hope.
Eulalia Bernard, Costa Rican poet

For any man without woman there is not heaven in the sky or on earth. Without woman there would be no sun, no moon, no agriculture and no fire.
Muslim proverb

One thing is plain. If women do not put their freedom first, noone else will do so.
The Suffragist (British women's suffrage magazine) 1916

When you're a black woman, you seldom get to do what you just want to do; you always do what you have to do.
Dorothy I Height, president of the US National Council of Negro Women

In search of my mother's garden I found my own.
Alice Walker (1944-) US writer

If it were customary to send little girls to school and to teach them the same subjects as are taught to boys, they would learn just as fully and would understand the subtleties of all arts and sciences. Indeed, maybe they would understand them better… for just as women's bodies are softer than men's, so their understanding is sharper.
Christine de Pisan (c1363-1430) French writer

Heroines
WOMEN

My mother taught me to stir in the sugar before giving my husband the cup. But in the last six months we have learnt many things. Before, we thought it was impolite to let the man pour the tea. But that is changing.
Hissa al-Shaheen, Kuwaiti feminist, writing in 1991

That little man says women can't have as much rights as men, 'cause Christ wasn't a woman! Where did your Christ come from? Where did your Christ come from? From God and a woman! Man had nothing to do with Him.
Sojourner Truth (1797-1883) US slave and abolitionist

Women of Africa,
What are you not?
Okot p'Bitek, Ugandan poet

Failing to be there when a man wants her is a woman's greatest sin, except to be there when he doesn't want her.
Helen Rowland (1876-1950) US writer

A woman's work is never done by men!
Graffiti

South African women are finding their voices. Those voices need to boom out so that women can seize the moment and reap the benefits that their newly-won democracy has to offer.
Ferial Haffajee, contemporary South African journalist

Whatever women do, they must do it twice as well as men to be thought half as good. Luckily this is not difficult.
Charlotte Whitton (d 1975) Canadian politician

No woman can call herself free who does not own and control her body. No woman can call herself free until she can choose consciously whether she will or will not be a mother.
Margaret Sanger (1883-1966) US pioneer of the family planning movement

Whether women are better than men I cannot say - but I can say they are certainly no worse.
Golda Meir (1898-1978) Israeli prime minister

I feel very angry when I think of brilliant or even interesting women whose minds are wasted on a home. Better have an affair. It isn't so permanent and you keep your job.
JK Galbraith (1908-) Canadian-born economist

Terms of endearment
LOVE AND FRIENDSHIP

Love is a secret which cannot be revealed,
But by two hundred curtains it cannot be concealed.
Jami (1414-1492) Persian poet

Accept others with tolerance,
be positive and far-sighted in your
endeavours, and you can be
impartial and balanced in action.
Anon

You were
water to me
deep and bold and fathoming.
Grace Nichols (1950-) Guyanan writer

For news of the heart, ask the face.
Hausa proverb, Nigeria

There's no way to repay a mother's
love, or lack of it.
Mignon McLaughlin, contemporary US writer

Most human beings are quite likeable
if you do not see too much of them.
Robert Lynd (1879-1949) Irish writer

To be a demographer's friend
Is really no use in the end
For she's given her heart
To a graph and a chart
And she lives with a nice-looking trend.
Lord Caradon, British politician, at the 1974 World
Population Conference in Bucharest

The shortest distance between two
people is a smile.
Anon

Before I got married I had six theories about bringing up children; now I have six children and no theories.

JOHN WILMOT, EARL OF ROCHESTER (1647-1680)

71

Terms of endearment
LOVE AND FRIENDSHIP

I was married when I was 18. I was betrothed when I was 13. My husband was then 14. It was our parents who decided it, but we were shown to each other and accepted it. I have never thought of anyone else.
Li Yang-ching, Chinese woman

lovin wasn easy all de time
sweet
but nat easy
some a de time
Jean Binta Breeze, Jamaican poet

The institution of marriage must have been invented by an unimaginative pig.
Albert Einstein (1879-1955) German-born physicist

Talking with one another is loving one another.
Kenyan proverb

The air between us is like glass when we speak, our words frost.
Kendel Hippolyte (1952-   ) St Lucian poet

In the end we will conserve only what we love; we will love only what we understand.
Dioum, Baba of Senegal

The only way to have a friend is to be one.
Anon

Terms of endearment
LOVE AND FRIENDSHIP

Brother mine, treat not our mother in this
fashion,
'Twas us two that she fed at her two breasts,
'Tis to us two that she gives whatever she has,
Worship her as you would worship the
Buddha.
Sri Lankan folk-song

Macho does not prove mucho.
Zsa Zsa Gabor (1919-   ) US actress

The diversity of the human family
should be the cause of love and
harmony, as it is in music where many
different notes blend together in the
making of a perfect chord.
Baha'u'llah (1817-1892) founder of the Baha'i faith

I like me black face
And me kinky hair.
But nobody loves dem,
I jes don't tink it's fair.
Una Marson (1905-1965) Jamaican writer

Hate the sin and love the sinner.
Mohandas K Gandhi (1869-1948) Indian
nationalist leader

Where have you gone
with your confident
walk your
crooked smile the
rent money
in one pocket and
my heart
in another...
Mari E Evans (1923-   )
US poet

A good horse is a
member of the family.
Quashgai saying, Iran

73

Terms of endearment
LOVE AND FRIENDSHIP

Absence extinguishes small passions and increases great ones, as the wind will blow out a candle, and blow in a fire.
Duc de La Rochefoucauld (1613-1680) French writer

There is only one happiness in life, to love and be loved.
George Sand (1804-1876) French writer

Love one another, but make not a bond of love.
Let it rather be a moving sea between the shores of your souls.
Kahlil Gibran (1833-1967) Lebanese poet

Before I got married I had six theories about bringing up children; now I have six children and no theories.
John Wilmot (1647-1680) Earl of Rochester

Do not use a hatchet to remove a fly from your friend's forehead.
Chinese proverb

Don't walk behind me
I may not lead.
Don't walk in front of me
I may not follow.
Walk beside me
And be my friend.
Anon

Each family has its own football team.
Comment on family size from the Maghreb, North Africa

In the arithmetic of love, one plus one equals everything, and two minus one equals nothing.
Mignon McLaughlin, contemporary US writer

Home is not where you live but where they understand you.
Anon

People are not heterosexual or homosexual, just sexual.
Quentin Crisp (1908-) contemporary British critic and writer

The only abnormality is the incapacity to love.
Anais Nin (1903-1977) French-born writer and feminist

Do not protect yourself by a fence but rather by your friends.
Czech proverb

I conceived at least one great love in my life, of which I was always the object.
Albert Camus (1913-1960) French existentialist writer

Love thy neighbour as thyself, but choose your neighbourhood.
Louise Beal

It is difficult to get by if there is no love in the family.
Rahima Khatun, village woman in Bangladesh

River deep, mountain high
ENVIRONMENT

Mosquitos
Are the fattest
Inhabitants
Of this republic.
Fred D'Aguiar (1960-)
Guyanan writer

No person should have more land
than they need for dignified
sustenance. Who can dispute the
fact that the grinding poverty of the
masses is due to their having no
land that they can call their own?
Mohandas K Gandhi (1869-1948) Indian
nationalist leader

I like trees because they seem more
resigned to the way they have to live
than other things do.
Willa Cather (1873-1947) US writer

People are organic with the world. The
inner life moulds the environment and
is itself also deeply affected by it. The
one acts upon the other and every
abiding change in the life of a person is
the result of these mutual reactions.
Shoghi Effendi (1897-1957) great-grandson of
Baha'u'llah (1817-1892), founder of the Baha'i faith

This society has more comfort, safety
and power than any before it, but the
quality of life is cheapened by the
physical and emotional junk heap we
have created.
René Dubos (1901-1982) French agriculturist and
writer

How can the spirit of the earth like the
White man? Everywhere the White man
has touched it, it is sore.
Wintu Native American woman

Mosquitos
Are the fattest
Inhabitants
Of this Republic

FRED D'AGUIAR (1960-)
GUYANAN WRITER

River deep, mountain high

ENVIRONMENT

Forests precede civilizations, deserts follow them.

Vicomte de Chateaubriand (1768-1848) French diplomat and writer

This land is the place where we know where to find all that it provides for us - food from hunting and fishing, and farms, building tools and medicine.

The Akawaio Indians in Guyana, protesting about their removal for a hydro-electric dam project

Disturbing sacred sites and land is agony for our people. Land and mountains and spring water - the heart of the sacred sites - is really our body.

David Mowaljarlai, Australian aboriginal land-rights activist

The great sea
has set me adrift
It moves me
As the weed in a great river
Earth and the great weather
Move me
Have carried me away
And move my inward parts with joy.

Uvavnuk, Canadian Inuit woman

We use 30 per cent of the world's energy... That isn't bad, that is good. That means we are the richest, strongest people in the world.

Richard Nixon (1913-1994) US president

River deep, mountain high
ENVIRONMENT

We did not think of the open plains, the beautiful rolling hills and the winding streams as 'wild'. To us it was tame... We were surrounded with the blessings of the Great Mystery.
Chief Luther Standing Bear, Oglala Lakota Native American

Worms have played a more important part in the history of the world than humans would at first suppose.
Charles Darwin (1809-1882) British naturalist

Social forestry: the rich get richer and the poor get seedlings.
Community forestry: both rich and poor get poorer and no-one gets seedlings.
Traditional forestry: the rich get richer and no-one worries about the poor or the seedlings.
Anon

From these days [of country childhood] I date my love of the veld, of open spaces, the simple beauties of nature, the clean line of the horizon.
Nelson Mandela (1918-) first black president of South Africa

I'd rather wake up in the middle of nowhere than in any city on earth.
Steve McQueen (1930-1980) US film actor

We must learn to look at nature as something sacred... or we will have no future.
José Lutzenberger, ecologist and former Brazilian Minister of the Environment

If we give you our Land, please teach your children what we have taught our children... that the earth is our Mother.
Chief Seattle, Chief of the Dwamish Native Americans

79

River deep, mountain high
ENVIRONMENT

Hills are always more beautiful than stone buildings. Living in a city is an artificial existence. Lots of people hardly ever feel real soil under their feet, see plants grow except in flower pots, or get far enough beyond the street light to catch the enchantment of a night sky studded with stars.

Tatanga Mani (Walking Buffalo) (1871-1967)
Stoney Native American

The land makes everybody one. It determines relationships between clans in their social life as well as in their spiritual life.

Rrurrambu Dhurrkay, Australian
aboriginal writer

The Middle Ages may have been a time of salutary delay. If it had exploited the earth's surface as we are doing, we would perhaps not be around at all.

Jakob Burckhardt (1818-1897)

Human beings were invented by water as a device for transporting itself from one place to another.

Tom Robbins (1936-) US writer

Land monopoly is not the only monopoly which exists, but it is by far the greatest of monopolies - it is a perpetual monopoly, and it is the mother of all other forms of monopoly.

Winston Churchill (1874-1965)
British prime minister

Developing stations in outer space or on the bottom of oceans will not modify significantly, if at all, the limitations of human life. Humanity emerged on the earth, evolved under its influence, was shaped by it, and biologically is bound to it forever. People may dream of stars and engage in casual flirtations with other worlds, but they will remain wedded to the earth, their sole source of sustenance.
René Dubos (1901-1982) French agriculturist and writer

The earth provides enough to satisfy every man's need but not enough for every man's greed.
Mohandas K Gandhi (1869-1948) Indian nationalist leader

Until the lions have their historians, tales of hunting will always glorify the hunter.
African saying

We do not inherit the earth from our fathers; we borrow it from our children.
Native American saying, seen on bridge on the route of the Newbury by-pass, England

When the earth has been ravaged and the animals are dying, a tribe of people from all races, creeds and colours will put their faith in deeds, not words, to make the land green again. They will be called warriors of the rainbow, protectors of the environment.
Eyes of Fire, a Cree Native American woman

River deep, mountain high
ENVIRONMENT

We need nature more than nature needs us.

Sadruddin Aga Khan, spiritual leader of the Ismaili sect of Shi'a Muslims, in 1991

Those who make private property of the Gift of God, pretend in vain to be innocent. For in thus retaining the subsistence of the poor, they are the murderers of those who die every day for want of it.

Pope Gregory I (540-604)

There is one earth but many worlds.

Mercy Oduyoye, Ghana

What white people do for sport and recreation, we do for life - for the life of our bodies, for the life of our spirits, and for the life of our ancient culture. We caught our annual first fish, the traditional delight of all, but it got sent to the state to be tested for oil. We walk our beaches. But instead of gathering life we gather death. Dead birds. Dead otters. Dead seaweed. Never in the millennium of our tradition have we thought it possible for the water to die. But it is true.

Walter Aganeck, Native American, on the 1989 Exxon Valdez oil spill in Alaska

We borrow environmental capital from future generations with no intention or prospect of repaying.

World Commission on Environment and Development

The sky is held
up by the trees.
Native American saying

Land belongs to one large family, few of whom are alive, many of whom are dead, countless of whom are yet unborn.
Dr RS Mogoba, on African land tenure, 1992

I say to you, take care of this great wilderness as if it were your own garden. For in this place will grow the peace and knowledge that we will use in order to survive.
Will Steger (1944-) US Arctic traveller

Like the grass each spring we are transformed:
Our hearts grow green put forth their shoots.
Brazilian Indian leader

What my child learns of the sea
of the summer thunder
Of the bewildering riddle that hides
at the vortex of spring
She will learn in my twilight
And childlike
Revise every autumn.
Audre Lorde (1934-1992) US writer

This we know. The earth does not belong to us; we belongs to the earth... Whatever befalls the earth befalls the children of the earth. We did not weave the web of life; we are merely a strand in it. Whatever we do to the web, we do to ourselves.
Chief Seattle, Chief of the Dwamish Native Americans

Trees are the earth's endless effort to speak to the listening heavens.
Rabindranath Tagore (1861-1941)
Bengali Nobel Prizewinning poet

River deep, mountain high
ENVIRONMENT

To breath clean air
to drink pure water to plant new crops
to soak up the rain to wash off the stink
to hold this body and soul together in
peace
that's it
Push back the catastrophes.

Jayne Cortez (1936-) US poet

Reduce your wants
and supply your needs.

Mohandas K Gandhi (1869-1948)
Indian nationalist leader

Over increasingly large areas of the
United States, spring now comes
unheralded by the return of the birds,
and the early mornings are strangely
silent where once they were filled with
the beauty of bird song.

Rachel Carson (1907-1964) US writer and biologist

White people came here a long time
ago; took all the furs; trapped all the
beaver out; and the otter and the mink,
things like that; and they gathered all
these things up. They went away and
they left us with the bush and the rocks.
It wasn't too much later they came back
again. They call that logging. Cut down
all the trees; white pine, red pine, cut it
all down. And they left us on the bare
rocks. Then they discovered uranium
here. And the old man said, 'Now the
sons-a-bitches are back for the rocks'.

Gilbert Oskaboose, Serpent River Band

We spray the fields and scatter
The poison on the ground,
So that no wicked wild flowers
Upon our farms are found.

John Betjeman (1906-1984) British poet

A tree's a tree. How many more do you
want to look at? If you've seen one,
you've seen them all.

Ronald Reagan (1911-) US president

Sell a country! Why not sell the air, the great sea, as well as the earth? Did not the Great Spirit make them all for the use of his children? How can we have confidence in the white people?

Tecumseh (Shooting Star) Shawnee chief, in 1810, rejecting land purchases

We won't have a society if we destroy the environment.

Margaret Mead (1901-1978) US anthropologist

The flowers which fall from the tree are to prepare the land for new and more beautiful flowers to bloom in the next season.

Samora Machel (1933-1986) first president of Mozambique

Do you know that trees talk? Well they do. They talk to each other, and they'll talk to you if you listen... I have learned a lot from trees: sometimes about the weather, sometimes about animals, sometimes about the Great Spirit.

Tatanga Mani (Walking Buffalo) (1871-1967) Stoney Native American

Enjoy the earth gently
For if the earth is spoiled
It cannot be repaired
Enjoy the earth gently
Yoruba poem, Nigeria

Men argue, nature acts.
François Voltaire (1694-1778) French philosopher

River deep, mountain high
ENVIRONMENT

Only when the last tree has died
and the last river been poisoned
and the last fish been caught
will we realise that we cannot eat money.
Chief Seattle, Chief of the Dwamish Native Americans

The sky is our village umbrella.
If you tear the portion above your roof,
There will be rain-water in my inner
rooms.
Niyi Osundare, Nigerian poet

What do the forests bear?
Soil, water and pure air.
Slogan of Chipko, the Indian environmental
movement

We can do noble acts without ruling
the earth and sea.
Aristotle (322-264BC) Greek philosopher and
scientist

After you have exhausted
what there is in business, politics,
conviviality, and so on - have found
that none of these finally satisfy, or
permanently wear - what remains?
Nature remains.
Walt Whitman (1819-1892) US poet

We are fighting to defend the forest.
It is because the forest is what makes
us, and what makes our hearts go.
Because without the forest we won't be
able to breathe and our hearts will
stop and we will die.
Paiakan and Kube, Kayapo Indian leaders, Brazil

All there is lives on all there is...
Kahlil Gibran (1883-1931) Lebanese poet

Everything that we Indians weave is related to nature: eagles, horses, volcanoes, birds... things like that. We don't weave anything else.
Elena, Ixil Indian weaver from Guatemala

Holy Mother Earth, the trees and all nature are witnesses of your thoughts and deeds.
Winnebago Native American saying

Nature is only an immense ruin.
Paul Claudel (d 1955) French composer

We love quiet; we suffer the mouse to play; when the woods are rustled by the wind, we fear not.
Native American chief to the governor of Pennsylvania, 1796

In the eyes of Nature we are just another species in trouble.
Lionel Tiger and **Robin Fox**, contemporary British anthropologists

If sunbeams were weapons of war, we would have had solar power long ago.
George Porter (1902-) British chemist

The Arctic expresses the sum of all wisdom: silence.
Walter Bauer

Nature composes some of its loveliest poems for the microscope and telescope.
Theodore Roszak (1933-) US cultural thinker and writer

Free speech
STRUGGLE AND FREEDOM

My place is in the sunlight of opportunity.
Martin Luther King Jr (1929-1968)
US civil rights leader

Loyalty to petrified opinion never yet broke a chain or freed a human soul.
Mark Twain (1835-1910) US writer

I know why the caged bird sings.
Maya Angelou (1928-) US writer

We are this beacon of hope for the world because we are so improbable.
Archbishop Desmond Tutu (1931-) on South Africa's prospects at the first free elections in 1994

Power to the People.
1968 slogan of the US Black Panther movement

All human beings are born free and equal in dignity and in rights.
Universal Declaration of Human Rights, 1948

The moment the slave resolves that he will not longer be a slave, his fetters fall. He frees himself and shows the way to others. Freedom and slavery are mental states.
Mohandas K Gandhi (1869-1948) Indian nationalist leader

In a consumer society there are inevitably two kinds of slaves: the prisoners of addiction and the prisoners of envy.
Ivan Illich (1926-) US sociologist

I sit on a man's back choking him and making him carry me, and yet assure myself and others that I am sorry for him and wish to lighten his load by all means...except for getting off his back

LEO TOLSTOY (1828–1910) RUSSIAN WRITER

Free speech
STRUGGLE AND FREEDOM

Half a loaf eaten in freedom is better than a whole loaf eaten in slavery.

Anon

No pasaran! (They shall not pass!)

Dolores Ibarruri (1898-1989) Spanish republican revolutionary known as 'La Pasionaria', during the civil war

Lay down your weapons. Be wise… Though the whites exterminate the trunk they cannot pull out the roots.

Te Whiti, New Zealand/Aotearoa Maori pacifist leader, c1872

We gotta get out while we're young, 'Cause tramps like us baby, we were born to run.

Bruce Springsteen (1949-   ) US rock singer

The dignity of a people depends on how it treats a minority.

Kumar Rupesinghe, Sri Lankan activist

I have never been contained Except I made the prison.

Mari Evans (1923-   ) US writer

Long years ago we made a tryst with destiny, and now the time comes when we shall redeem our pledge… At the stroke of the midnight hour, when the world sleeps, India will awaken to life and freedom.

Jawaharlal Nehru (1889-1964) first prime minister of India

Free speech

I guess the secret of my youth is struggle.
Miriam Makeba, South African singer and activist

Make a career of humanity. Commit yourself to the noble struggle for equal rights. You will make a greater person of yourself, a greater nation of your country, and a finer world to live in.
Martin Luther King (1929-1968) US civil rights leader

We shall fight forever.
Maori social justice slogan, New Zealand/Aotearoa

I sit on a man's back choking him and making him carry me, and yet assure myself and others that I am sorry for him and wish to lighten his load by all means... except for getting off his back.
Leo Tolstoy (1828-1910) Russian writer

I have never regretted my commitment to the struggle, and I was always prepared to face the hardships that affected me personally. But my family paid a terrible price, perhaps too dear a price, for my commitment.
Nelson Mandela (1918-   ) first black president of South Africa

Freedom is the right to choose the bars of your own cage.
Anon

While the State exists, there is no freedom. When there is freedom there will be no State.
VI Lenin (1870-1924) Russian revolutionary leader

Free speech
STRUGGLE AND FREEDOM

Freedom is nothing else but a chance to be better.
Albert Camus (1913-1960) French existentialist writer

Those who expect to reap the blessings of freedom must undergo the fatigue of supporting it.
Thomas Paine (1737-1809) British thinker

If Negro freedom is taken away, or that of any minority group, the freedom of all the people is taken away.
Paul Robeson (1898-1976) US singer and political activist

To enjoy freedom we have to control ourselves.
Virginia Woolf (1882-1941) British writer

Education is our passport to the future, for tomorrow belongs to the people who prepare for it today.
Malcolm X (1925-1965) Black Muslim activist

Freedom is the real source of human happiness and creativity. Only when it is allowed to flourish can a genuinely stable international climate exist.
Dalai Lama (1931-) Tibetan spiritual leader

Revolution is the festival of the oppressed.
Germaine Greer (1939-) Australian-born writer

Soon must come the day
When the righteous have their way.
Unjustly tried are freed.
Tracy Chapman, contemporary US singer

It was enjoyable to sit in the shade... and sleep the sleep of liberty.
Aline França (1949-) Brazilian writer

I was born free - free in every way that I could know. Free to run in the fields near my mother's hut, free to swim in the clear stream that ran through my village, free to roast mealies under the stars and ride the broad back of slow-moving bulls.
Nelson Mandela (1918-) first black president of South Africa

Never doubt that a small group of thoughtful committed citizens can change the world; indeed it's the only thing that ever has.
Margaret Mead (1901-1978) US anthropologist

Emancipate yourselves from mental slavery.
None but ourselves can free our minds.
Bob Marley (1945-1981) Jamaican reggae singer

We shall have to repent in this generation not so much for the evil deeds of the wicked people but for the appalling silence of the good people.
Martin Luther King (1929-1968) US civil rights leader

You cannot know how long we cried until we laughed over the broken pieces of our dreams.
Abena PA Busia (1953-) Ghanaian-born writer

Free speech
STRUGGLE AND FREEDOM

Moving from silence into speech is for the oppressed, the colonized, the exploited, and those who stand and struggle side by side a gesture of defiance that heals, that makes new life and new growth possible.

bell hooks (1952-) US writer

Change is within the land, as if the Earth were pregnant, full of this new life, and the time has arrived to give birth.

Elda Broilo, Movement of Landless Rural Workers, Brazil

Rise like lions after slumber
In unvanquishable number,
Shake your chains to earth like dew
Which in sleep had fallen on you
Ye are many - they are few.

PB Shelley (1792-1822) British poet

The world changed from trouble to kisses.

Gayl Jones (1949-) US writer

The hope of the world is still in dedicated minorities. The trail-blazers in human scientific and religious freedom have always been in a minority.

Martin Luther King (1929-1968) US civil rights leader

We are the rainbow people of God, and we are unstoppable, black and white, as we move together to freedom.

Archbishop Desmond Tutu (1931-) on South Africa's future

Free speech
STRUGGLE AND FREEDOM

No dynamic golden pill is ever going to solve our human problems. They can be solved only by bringing about a radical revolution in the mind and the heart of man. This demands hard, constant work, seeing and listening, and thus being highly sensitive.

Jiddu Krishnamurti (1895-1986)
Indian philosopher

Philosophers have sought to interpret the world: the point however is to change it.

Karl Marx (1818-1883) German philosopher and revolutionary

Make me a grave where'er you will,
In a lowly plain or a lofty hill;
Make it among earth's humblest graves,
But not in a land where people are slaves.

Frances EW Harper (1825-1911) child of freed slaves

It is better to die on your feet
than live on your knees.

Emiliano Zapata (1879-1919) Mexican revolutionary

First they came for the Jews
and I did not speak out -
because I was not a Jew.
Then they came for the communists
and I did not speak out -
because I was not a communist.
Next they came for the trade unionists
and I did not speak out -
because I was not a trade unionist.
Then they came for me
and there was no-one left
to speak out for me.

Pastor Niemoller, used in Minority Rights/New Internationalist poster

Spilt blood is not roots of trees
But it is the closest to roots
human beings have.

Yehuda Amichai,
contemporary Israeli poet

Free speech
STRUGGLE AND FREEDOM

Write down
I am an Arab
I am a name without a family name

Mahmoud Darwish, contemporary Palestinian poet

I have cherished the ideal of a democratic and free society... it is an ideal which I hope to live for and to achieve. But if need be it is an ideal for which I am prepared to die.

Nelson Mandela (1918-) first black president of South Africa

My silence is very noisy. Nothing and no-one can silence my spirit. There are no boundaries or prisons to the human spirit. I am still alive.

Mordechai Vanunu, Israeli dissident

I had heard that in Los Angeles, gay people can live free from persecution. It was my dream to come to the US where I could live freely.

Sergey Fedetov, a Russian from a small town near Moscow, who was beaten, interrogated and jailed by officialdom

Right in the centre of our lives liberty shines,
begets our race
and sows the salt of words.

Andrée Chedid (1921-) Egyptian writer

Many will call me an adventurer, and I am, but of a different kind - one who risks his skin in order to prove his convictions.

Ernesto Che Guevara (1928-1967) Argentinian doctor and revolutionary

Free speech
STRUGGLE AND FREEDOM

The man in chains, seeing another man without them, thinks: Is it possible I could have struck these chains off if I had only tried, that I didn't have to wear them all these years? The thought is unbearable. Better get some chains on the other guy.

John Holt (1923-1985) US educator

No force can now stop or even delay our emancipation from the pain and shame of our racist past.

Judge Ismail Mohamed on South Africa's moves to a new constitution

Keep your eyes on the prize.

US civil rights movement song

Let me be free - free to travel, free to stop, free to follow the trade where I choose, free to choose my own teachers, free to follow the religion of my father, free to think, talk and act for myself, and I will obey every law or submit to the penalty...

Chief Joseph, Nez Percé Native American

Blood, toil, tears and sweat
WORK

One machine can do the work of 50 ordinary people. No machines can do the work of one extraordinary person.
Elbert Hubbard (1859-1915) US writer

Forty years in the factory,
Thirty years on the bus,
Twenty years with machinery,
They don't make them any
more like us.
Marsha Prescod (1950s-   )
Trinidad-born writer

The work, my friend, is peace.
Franklin D Roosevelt (1882-1945) US president, in a 1945 address

One of the symptoms of approaching nervous breakdown is the belief that one's work is terribly important, and that to take a holiday would bring all kinds of disaster.
Bertrand Russell (1872-1970) British philosopher

I like work: it fascinates me. I can sit and look at it for hours.
Jerome K Jerome (1859-1927) British writer

Hungry people have no respect for law, authority, or human life.
Marcus Garvey (1887-1940) Jamaican-born black nationalist

The workers have nothing to lose but their chains. They have a world to gain. Workers of the world, unite.
Karl Marx (1818-1883) German revolutionary thinker

Some are bent with toil,
and some get crooked trying to avoid it.
HERBERT V PROCHNOW

Blood, toil, tears and sweat
WORK

I sleep and work. I can do nothing else.
Woman worker in Mexican *maquiladora* (sweatshop), 1994

It is difficult to go on strike if there is no work in the first place.
Lord George-Brown (1914-1985) British politician

Young people ought not to be idle. It is very bad for them.
Margaret Thatcher (1925-) British prime minister

I was nine or ten when I came to work for the first time. I was working... as a day labourer, weeding, watching and the like... When next year comes I'll return as a harvester. I'll know how to cut cane.
Bolivian sugar-cane cutter, aged 14

It's been a hard day's night
And I've been working like a dog.
Beatles song, A Hard Day's Night

Some are bent with toil, and some get crooked trying to avoid it.
Herbert V Prochnow

Rest is the sauce of labour.
Plutarch (c125 AD) Greek philosopher and politician

Television is a device that permits people who haven't anything to do to watch people who can't do anything.
Fred Allen (1894-1956) US humorist

You cannot use yesterday's tools for today's job and expect to be in business tomorrow.
Prof Fafunwa, Nigeria

Blood, toil, tears and sweat
WORK

It is impossible to enjoy idling thoroughly unless one has plenty of work to do. There is no fun in doing nothing when you have nothing to do.
Jerome K Jerome (1859-1927) British writer

If everybody lived by the sweat of their brow, the earth would become a paradise.
Mohandas K Gandhi (1869-1948) Indian nationalist leader

By his very success in inventing labour-saving devices modern man has manufactured an abyss of boredom that only the privileged classes in earlier civilisations have ever fathomed.
Lewis Mumford (1895-1990) US social philosopher

Work is love made visible.
Kahlil Gibran (1883-1931) Lebanese poet

Tote dat barge, heave dat bale,
Get a little drunk and you land in jail.
Jerome Kern (1885-1945) US songwriter

My young men shall never work. Men who work cannot dream, and wisdom comes in dreams.
Smohalla, Nez Percé Native American

What the country needs are a few labor-making inventions.
Arnold Glasgow

How beautiful it is to do nothing, and then rest afterwards.
Spanish proverb

We shape our tools and thereafter our tools shape us.
Marshall McLuhan (1911-1980) Canadian sociologist

Forked tongue
THEY REALLY SAID IT!

It is good things like this war that help to take people's minds off irrelevant issues like the environment.
Margaret Thatcher (1925-) British prime minister, during the 1982 Malvinas/Falklands war

My government will protect all liberties but one - the liberty to do away with other liberties.
Gustavo Diaz Ordaz (1911-) Mexican president

I'd like to extend a warm welcome to Chairman Mo.
Ronald Reagan (1911-) US president, greeting then President Doe of Liberia

I asked a Burmese why women, after centuries of following their men, now walk in front. He said there were many unexploded landmines since the war.
Anon

I love criticism just so long as it's unqualified praise.
Noel Coward (1899-1973) British playwright

The expansion of the right of the individual to behave or misbehave as he pleases has come at the expense of an orderly society.
Lee Kuan Yew (1923-) prime minister of Singapore

The thing is to be able to outlast the trends.
Paul Anka (1941-) US popsinger

Feminism encourages women to leave their husbands, kill their children, practice witchcraft, destroy capitalism and become lesbians.
Pat Robertson, US religious-right politician, in 1992

102

I asked a Burmese why women, after centuries of following their men, now walk in front? He said there were many unexploded landmines since the war.
ANON

Forked tongue
THEY REALLY SAID IT!

Here lies Captain Ernest Bloomfield. Accidentally shot by his orderly, March 2nd 1897. "Well done, thou good and faithful servant".

Inscription on imperial gravestone, Peshawar, North West Frontier, Pakistan

I drink to make other people interesting.
George Jean Nathan (1882-1958) US critic

The ANC is a typical terrorist organisation… Anyone who thinks it is going to run the government in South Africa is living in cloud-cuckoo-land.
Margaret Thatcher (1925-) British prime minister

Perfection is such a nuisance that I often regret having cured myself of tobacco.
Emile Zola (1840-1902) French writer

When I went to America I had two secretaries, one for autographs, and other for locks of hair. Within six months the one had died of writer's cramp, the other was completely bald.
Oscar Wilde (1854-1900) Irish-born playwright

There are some days when I think I'm going to die from an overdose of satisfaction.
Salvador Dali (1904-1989) Spanish painter

A single death is a tragedy, a million deaths is a statistic.
Joseph Stalin (1879-1953) Soviet communist leader

Forked tongue
THEY REALLY SAID IT!

Kill one person and you are a murderer,
Kill millions and you are a conqueror,
Kill all, and you are a god.
Anon

Universities have created all our miseries. Universities do more damage than cluster bombs.
Ayatollah Khomeini (1902-1989) spiritual leader of Iran

Well, I learnt a lot. You'd be surprised. They're all individual countries.
Ronald Reagan (1911-) US president, after his 1982 tour of South America

Anyone who sees and paints a sky green and pastures blue ought to be sterilized.
Adolf Hitler (1889-1945) German Nazi leader

I do not rule Russia - ten thousand clerks do.
Nicholas I (1796-1855) tsar of Russia

I don't see why we have to stand by and watch a country go Communist due to the irresponsibility of its own people.
Dr Henry Kissinger (1923-) US politician, on the election of Chilean Marxist president Salvador Allende in 1970

Voters quickly forget what a man says.
Richard Nixon (1913-1994) US president

We don't sit there every morning and say, 'How can we ruin a country?'
James Wolfensohn, president of the World Bank

Forked tongue
THEY REALLY SAID IT!

I don't feel we did wrong in taking this great country away from [the Indians]. There were great numbers of people who needed new land, and the Indians were selfishly trying to keep it for themselves.
John Wayne (1907-1979) US film star

We are not going to tolerate these attacks from outlaw states run by the strangest collection of misfits, looney tunes and squalid criminals since the Third Reich.
Ronald Reagan (1911-) US president, on Nicaragua's Sandinista government of the 1980s

All witchcraft comes from carnal lust, which in women is insatiable.
In *Malleus Maleficarum*, the investigation of witchcraft commissioned by Pope Innocent VIII in 1484

It is not impossible to rule Italians, but it would be useless.
Benito Mussolini (1883-1945) Italian fascist leader

The music of a well-ordered age is calm and cheerful and so is its government. The music of a restive age is excited and fierce, and its government is perverted.
Lu Pu-We, Chinese philosopher

No-one would remember the Good Samaritan if he only had good intentions He had money as well.
Margaret Thatcher (1925-) British prime minister

Forked tongue
THEY REALLY SAID IT!

I reject the cynical view that politics is inevitably, or even usually, a dirty business.
Richard Nixon (1913-1994) US president, in 1973

A bad thing has been turned into a good thing.
Jiang Zemin, Chinese president, saying the 1989 Tiananmen massacre led to stability and faster economic reform

We will bury you.
Nikita Khruschev (1894-1971) Soviet premier, speaking of the USA

An evil empire.
Ronald Reagan (1911-) US president, speaking of the Soviet Union

I wish I could bring Stonehenge to Malawi to show there was a time when Britain had a savage culture.
Hastings Banda (1906-) president of Malawi

Women when they are in power are much harsher than men. Much more cruel. Much more bloodthirsty. I'm quoting facts, not opinions.
Mohammed Reza Pahlevi (1919-1980) shah of Iran

I owe nothing to Women's Lib.
Margaret Thatcher (1925-) British prime minister

As far as criticism is concerned, we don't resent that unless it is absolutely biased, as it is in most cases.
John Vorster (1915-1983) South African prime minister

Forked tongue
THEY REALLY SAID IT!

I defy the allegations, and I defy the allegator.
Fred Gardiner, Toronto city politician

I am proud of democracy in the country and do not want to do anything against it.
Indira Gandhi (1917-1984) Indian prime minister, during the State of Emergency

The United States is the best and fairest and most decent nation on the face of the earth.
George Bush (1924-) US president

I have drained the poisoned chalice to the dregs.
Benito Mussolini (1883-1945) Italian fascist leader's last words

No one can kill Americans and brag about it. No one.
Ronald Reagan (1911-) US president

Guns will make us powerful; butter will only make us fat.
Hermann Goering (1893-1946) German Nazi politician

Forked tongue
THEY REALLY SAID IT!

Every communist must grasp the truth: political power grows out of the barrel of a gun.
Mao Zedong (1893-1976) Chinese communist leader

It is not the neutrals or the lukewarm who make history.
Adolf Hitler (1889-1945) German Nazi leader

Everything around here is financed by the French government. We ask the French for money, get it and waste it.
Jean Bédel Bokassa (1921-1996) president and self-styled emperor of the Central African Republic

I will continue to be the essence of sweet reasonableness.
Margaret Thatcher (1925-) British prime minister

About K rky

Korky Paul was born in Harare, Zimbabwe, in 1951 into a family of seven children. His real name is Hamish Vigne Christie Paul. He enjoyed a wild and privileged childhood in the African Bushveld. At an early age Korky was reading comic books and scribbling cartoons. Later he went to Durban School of Art and then to an advertising agency in Cape Town. Korky left South Africa in 1976 and worked as an illustrator first in Greece and then in London and Los Angeles. In 1980 his first children's book, *The Crocodile and Dumper Truck* was published. He illustrated *Winnie the Witch* which won the Children's Book Award in 1987, establishing Korky as one of today's most popular children's book illustrators.

Whatever you can do
or dream you can do, begin it.
Boldness has genius, power
and magic in it.
Begin it now.